POSITIVISM

LET THIS MIND BE IN YOU

POSITIVISM

LET THIS MIND BE IN YOU

EDDIE ROBINSON JR

Positivism
Edward Robinson, Jr.

A Gathering of the Ways
P.O. Box 23183
Richmond, Virginia 23223

Interior and Cover Designs by Edward Robinson, Jr.

Koa Publishing Company
P.O. Box 3203
Manassas, Virginia 20108

Library of Congress
Copyright © 2022 by Edward Robinson, Jr.
ISBN 979-8-9860577-0-5

Printed in the United States of America

POSITIVISM: A distinctive practice, a movement characterized by the presence or possession of features and qualities that are constructive and optimistic; good vibes...

-Eddie Robinson, Jr.

YOU ARE DIVINE BY DESIGN

YOUR ONLY LIMITATION IS

YOUR INDOCTRINATION AND YOUR

ONLY DISABILITY IS YOUR BELIEF

Everything in life is rooted in the MIND,

the power of our own thoughts.

Life is a result of what we believe.

Live what you believe.

The goal is to MASTER the MIND, to not live by circumstances

Thought becomes reality with FOCUS.

Condition the mind positively with POSITIVISM

Let this mind be in you

The internal war began with them and us and expanded from there

Proceed at your own pace.

Life is supposed to be fun.

ACKNOWLEDGMENTS

I AM forever grateful, and I want to express my sincere appreciation to the hundreds of you that receive my words of inspiration daily.

My journey is one of purposeful intentionality. I am encouraged by you to continue in the unseen journey that lies ahead. I would also like to thank Bridgette Williams of Koa Publishing Company for her collaboration in the challenging task of editing, organizing, and publishing this material for your enjoyment. She appeared in my life at this critical time with precise timing. Her presence and all the doors opening around me reminds me daily that I have decreed a thing coming to pass. With a front row seat, I watch it come to pass as all things must do with consistent/persistent focus. It's the law. And yet this too shall pass. It is also the law.

DEDICATION

This book is dedicated to you. Thank you for being here as I enter spiritual maturity. My eyes are fully open to see the splendor and joy of everyday living. The radiance of a hopeful humanity has sparked a glimmer in my eyes that I cannot deny. My longing for spiritual growth and expansion has lead me to go deep within to grasp hold of the parts of life that come into focus with depth. I am inspired, guided, and nurtured by my spirit. I am now able to live out of my CORE of BEING.

This day I have come to believe, whether it is a child, mother, father, sister, brother, or a significant other, love can be given to anyone, indiscriminately, because love has no form except the form you give it. Love comes from the inside out. I get to choose when, where, and how to give it. At the same time, I realize that the GOD/SOURCE of all is LOVE. So, if SOURCE is love and love is SOURCE and LOVE comes from within, then where SOURCE resides is within me. SOURCE resides in the core of my being. When two people come together from the awareness of their CORE of BEING, that is LOVE, it is the most powerful ENERGY on the planet. Serve LOVE and lose the ambiguity of GOD/SOURCE. LOVE conquers all.

PREFACE

I am writing this book to share my story, a story about being unwilling in some cases and willing in other areas to move forward. This book consists of reflections on the encounters, inspirational moments, and challenges I have faced along this life's path. One of my mentors inspired me to create a place where we could have a conversation about what we as human beings feel and face as common challenges. Of course, the indoctrinated rhetoric and dogma will always exist and persist, however this book is about our perceptions and allowing space for the mental conversation with ourselves. Life is about moving forward into the unseen aspects of reality. To understand what we don't know that we don't know. So, I am writing this book to have an energetic conversation within the confines of this book. I am attempting here to provoke thought and inner understanding as we all strive to move forward on our own.

I am indeed thankful and especially grateful for this journey I am embarking on with you. This book is about discovering your true SELF, to live in love, and to live complete individually. As you proceed, don't hesitate to ask yourself questions about your thoughts and how they became you. At the end of each passage, I have inserted this symbol (…) and the words "Pause" and "Reflect". When you see that, take your time to reflect and allow yourself to connect the text with your past or present. In this process you will optimize the value of each passage as it relates to you. You may feel the need to evaluate some of your thinking. The goal is to nourish your soul, not rush through courses.

POSITIVISM is the mind of SOURCE which supersedes all thought. Thoughts are things that already exist in the planet when we arrive. Join me as we explore some thoughts and dissect them. This is the place we have the conversation, within the confines of our own mind. This book is a guided conversation with our thoughts. Keep the thoughts positive.

The love vibration is the highest vibration. LIVE IN love. It is to live without fear, negativity, guilt, jealousy, and the ego's absolute need to defend itself at all costs.

Love is life affirming. I am good at love. I am the individualized force of SOURCE/God within and manifests my external reality through my thoughts. I am full of abundance in all areas of my life.

I welcome abundance and positive, life affirming people and events into my life now and always. I am thankful for the opportunity to be a branch of the tree of life and embrace all the benefits that come with that, unexpected infinite abundance, consciousness, and health.

I am made perfect, pure love, and the possibility of the magnificence of humanity.

I would also like to preface this writing by saying that god/source is everywhere, it begs to say then every path leads to god/SOURCE just as every path leads to your destiny, and the joint destiny of the planet. The current Western theory/theology of the god force comes out of the DARK AGES. The god force is everywhere, the ALL in ALL. The god force/SOURCE has two distinct sides that exist on the earth plane, consisting of both negative and positive energy. We have the free-will to decide which path you will follow. The only question that prevails is what is your path, which path creates for you and yours the expansion of consciousness?

Any theory about an external savior concludes that the god force/SOURCE is divine and I am not, therefore I need a barrier/savior/intercessor between me and the god force. But the god force resides in me, it recharges itself within me through the night, it keeps my heart beating, and lungs pumping. It is the breath of life. The soul (the individualized consciousness of the god force) is clothed in human flesh as man and woman, me! I AM DIVINE. Woman/Man is god asleep, god is man/woman awoke. Wake up! The divine energy/spiritual world is all about affirmative expansion, what you call the negative only comes to create balance. It rights the ship to get it back on an affirmative course. POSITIVISM is your ticket to the light whether you choose to accept it. It requires giving up a whole lot of the family and cultural indoctrination (in-dark-nation), reluctantly or freely.

The intention of this book is to actualize the human potential, to strive for the light, enlightenment. NAMASTE, in the Hindi tradition means the god/divinity in me acknowledges the divinity/god in you.

NAMASTE

Negative energy/thoughts if not transmuted will be transmitted or transferred

CONSCIOUSNESS IS MORE THAN ENOUGH

PAUSE

(…)

REFLECT

The intelligent management of human emotion through positivity carries you through any predicament. Our lives are defined by opportunity, even the ones we miss. "Opportunity will be mixed with difficulty," is the story of human history. Acquaint thine self with positivity. It is the energy of the divine self. It is not something you go after; positivity is an attitude. Opportunity is missed by most people because it's dressed in overalls and looks like work. Opportunities are never lost; someone will take the ones you miss. Not knowing when opportunity will come, I open every door. Positivism is the answer! Religion is positivism taught through the lens of culturally indoctrinated stories. Humpty Dumpty or Psalms. All we have to do is practice positivity. When David or any biblical character did something negative, negativity/suffering followed. Same with Goldie Locks and the Three Bears! When they did something positive, blessings followed no matter what their religious beliefs ? How many stories do you have to read to understand positivity means blessings and negativity means suffering? Know what you believe. Know what mama and daddy believe. Know what your holy book reads. Know what your master/mentor believes. All that matters for your ego (who you believe that you are). However, you should practice positivity and respect for what all people believe if we're going to live together. I believe in the positive flow of energy whereby

1

all parties involved in this thing called life gets a fair shake. I value all life: male or female, black or white, religion or no religion. Let's keep the vibration positive. The human race is the chosen people for this plane of existence. Any other belief is negative, separatism. All energy falls into two categories. It is either negative or positive. All is energy. Genocide is negative, whether initiated by Joshua, Hitler, or the British empire. If it ain't positive, keep it to yourself, and I don't care what your holy book says. Just as the word "water" does not make you wet, the words "god said" does not make one conscious. Positivism is the answer. I AM forever grateful. I can and will attract all things through my imagination (spiritual mind) that strengthens and guides me, by saying "YES" to life, living my intention, planting some beauty every day, and counting all costs. I AM, one creator (the individual authority over my life and decisions), one Soul (the individualized consciousness of source energy), made from one blood, one flesh, one spirit. I AM at ONE I and my creator. (SOURCE) are one. All is one. the Way of Consciousness

(…)

Life is inherently risky, count the cost. The cost of a thing is the amount of what I will call *life* which is required to be exchanged for it. Counting the cost involves looking at examples and asking yourself, "Am I prepared to face trials as a result of my beliefs and actions? Do I fully understand the ramifications of what I AM about to embark on?" "Counting the cost," means recognizing and agreeing to some terms first. It means to realize not what been lost, damaged or gained as a result of something but to project /envision the consequences of your desires before they are put into action. Can you manage your desires? Do you know and understand how to make room for them, or how to share in the responsibility of maintaining them? But how do you count the cost when you don't know what's coming? The answer is that it requires an upfront commitment to the highest possible cost. The true cost is knowing the value of what one does. Do the things that count. I AM forever grateful. I can and will attract all things through my imagination (spiritual mind) that strengthens and guides me, by saying "YES" to life, living my intention, planting some beauty every day, and counting all costs. I AM, one creator (the individual authority over my life and decisions), one Soul (the individualized consciousness of source energy), made from one blood, one flesh, one spirit. I AM at ONE I and my creator. (SOURCE) are one. All is one. the Way of Consciousness

(…)

We are responsible for what we are and whatever we wish ourselves to be. We have the power to make ourselves. If what we are now has been the result of our own past actions, it certainly follows that whatever we wish or wish to be in the future can be produced by our present actions.

Take care of this moment and tomorrow will take care of itself. The future is produced by our present actions. It is only a matter of time before our aspirations are realized, they are bound by effort. The gestation period of our wishes is bound by effort. Let's say you put in 1hour a day for 7 days or 7 hours in 1 day. Focus and attention to detail makes the thing you desire happen for you even faster, and as always you see in your mind it as already done. Live in the END. The gestation period is shortened by consistent and persistent effort. I AM forever grateful. I can and will attract all things through my imagination (spiritual mind) that strengthens and guides me, by saying "YES" to life, living my intention, planting some beauty every day, and counting all costs. I AM, one creator (the individual authority over my life and decisions), one Soul (the individualized consciousness of source energy), made from one blood, one flesh, one spirit. I AM at ONE I and my creator. (SOURCE) are one. All is one.
the Way of Consciousness

(…)

When things are going well, all is well. When we go to the movies the main character always faces some form of adversity, overcomes it, and we call it a great movie. She/he overcame! But how do you deal with life's adversity and challenges? Do you fight them ? Hurt people hurt people. Run away to the arms of the same challenge with a different DNA. Escape with isolation, eating and drinking disorders, drugs, or hatred. Is there any legitimate way to face adversity accept to dig a deep foundation that will withstand the wind, the rain, and the hailstorm? The fear that one resist persists comes from the inability to step up to the plate. Be present, challenges are only amplified in perceptions. Challenges become GIANTS in the land as espoused in the biblical allegory. It only looks like an obstacle, it's really a hurdle. "Whom do I say that I AM, in the face of adversity, an ant or a giant killer? It all relates to how we see ourselves. I AM bigger than any giant that was invented in my mind/perception. All is mind. I get to choose my thoughts. I can and will attract all things through my imagination (spiritual mind) that strengthens and guides me, by saying no to everything negative, creating some beauty every day, and counting all costs. I AM forever grateful. I can and will attract all things through my imagination (spiritual mind) that strengthens and guides me, by saying "YES" to life, living my intention, planting some beauty every day, and counting all costs. I AM, one creator (the individual authority over my life and decisions), one Soul (the individualized consciousness of source energy), made from one blood, one flesh, one spirit. I AM at ONE I and my creator. (SOURCE) are one. All is one.

the Way of Consciousness

(…)

You are not your status, nor your professional position. When the lights of a celebrity go out, who are you then? When you are no longer the president/leader of the club/social group or fraternity, who will you be then? What happens when you are no longer a means for the corporate end; no longer the center of

4

attention; no longer deserving of a private escort, a private plane, private parties; and no longer admired? Who are you then? You maybe "Black while driving, hash tag me too, or isolated in a nursing facility. Who are you after it is all said and done? A human being clothed in flesh, consisting of earth, air, water, and electricity. How will you use the resources that embody you? Every state that you have ever embodied, you have found to be true for you. You get to decide the form you shape as you create. I must learn the concepts of being/manifesting, magnifying that which I AM conscious of being that I might prepare my own place. I AM forever grateful. I can and will attract all things through my imagination (spiritual mind) that strengthens and guides me, by saying "YES" to life, living my intention, planting some beauty every day, and counting all costs. I AM, one creator (the individual authority over my life and decisions), one Soul (the individualized consciousness of source energy), made from one blood, one flesh, one spirit. I AM at ONE I and my creator. (SOURCE) are one. All is one.

the Way of Consciousness

(…)

Make a choice, choose a direction, and take the first step. Life has no guarantees for tomorrow with today being all that we have, and the most we can adhere to is a single direction. The direction is the place where a person is heading. The first step is to get out of your comfort zone and start acting. Notice what you truly enjoy doing. Look for inspiration and define success for yourself. Next comes the expansion. Everything in the universe expands. Nothing is as it used to be. The more you feel like you are assuming a new role, the more you feel terrified, the more you doubt yourself, and the more likely you're on the right track. You don't need to conquer fear. Act in spite of your fear. It's called courage. If you're pursuing something that doesn't scare you, it's not worth your time. Remember that it can be very difficult to get anywhere while you're starting off at the horizon. The key to finding direction is to put your feet on the ground and start exploring the options around you. Choose wisely. I AM forever grateful. I can and will attract all things through my imagination (spiritual mind) that strengthens and guides me, by saying "YES" to life, living my intention, planting some beauty every day, and counting all costs. I AM, one creator (the individual authority over my life and decisions), one Soul (the individualized consciousness of source energy), made from one blood, one flesh, one spirit. I AM at ONE I and my creator. (SOURCE) are one. All is one. the Way of Consciousness

(...)

True love is seen as the greatest energy of life in the unified field of consciousness. It is the most powerful healing energy, and it flows everywhere. Being able to channel the extraordinary power of love brings freedom from hate and from a host of other ills. Love can even bring freedom from disease, and our own basic selves. With love being the strongest emotion, a person can feel, add some passion and they together make for one hell of an unbreakable pairing. This passionate love energy is created by a cosmic bond for a special place in time. As it energizes the union and produces a flow of physical energy that feeds not only the physical body but the entire being. It produces the miracle of life. Rather than thinking of it as a state of mind, think of it as a state of divine energy that is created in a perfect union. Casual energy seekers are drawn to the individuals involved in this cosmic pairing as separate entities carrying individual pulls. Have you ever noticed that as soon as you commit to channel and focus the feeling that come from a cosmic union everyone wants a piece of you? Don't fool yourself. The unique attraction others feel is a magical expression of the union. Don't allow your flame to die out as others are drawn to your light by giving away that which is expressed as two become one. True love is a cosmic phenomenon. You don't seek it. It unfolds. I AM forever grateful. I can and will attract all things through my imagination (spiritual mind) that strengthens and guides me, by saying "YES" to life, living my intention, planting some beauty every day, and counting all costs. I AM, one creator

(the individual authority over my life and decisions), one Soul (the individualized consciousness of source energy), made from one blood, one flesh, one spirit. I AM at ONE I and my creator. (SOURCE) are one. All is one.
the Way of Consciousness

(…)

What are the laws and relations of the spiritual realm/kingdom of heaven? Much of the kingdom of heaven is explained biblically in terms that the outer man can grasp. It is likened unto a man that sewed good seeds in his field (mind) and the harvest came. The kingdom of heaven is the orderly adjustment of divine ideas planted in man's mind. Man/woman adjust their thoughts to the divine ideas by a process of denial by which inharmonious ideas are eliminated. Christ locates the kingdom heaven when he said, "The kingdom of heaven/god cometh not by observation, for lo the kingdom of god is within you!" It is harmony between the soul and the body, the inner and the outer man/woman. Plant into the mind a purpose, a path, a theme, something which moves you, one thing that you cannot be swayed from, that brings you energy, inspiration/happiness and all thing will be added to that focus. The mind is a magnet that will draw unto you all things similar to that which is established in it. It works much like YouTube adds. How can your path be added to if you haven't chosen a channel/path? Choose and it will define the next choice. You only have to get it right once. I AM forever grateful. I can and will attract all things through my imagination (spiritual mind) that strengthens and guides me, by saying "YES" to life, living my intention, planting some beauty every day, and counting all costs. I AM, one creator (the individual authority over my life and decisions), one Soul (the individualized consciousness of source energy), made from one blood, one flesh, one spirit. I AM at ONE I and my creator. (SOURCE) are one. All is one.
the Way of Consciousness

(…)

7

The I AM (your consciousness) is the only door in which things can come into the world for you. In the Christian tradition, manifestation comes through the father (SOURCE) upon my request through my imagination. I AM the way for that in which I desire to come into the world. How can anything I desire manifest except through me. I am the door to all that I desire by my thoughts. No one knows the process. The WAYS of the I AM are limitless. Consciousness (the father) will bring forth all that you ask whether rich or poor, Greek or Jew, bond or free, male or female. Why should you ask man when your world mirrors that in which you have imagined? You didn't imagine a business, you imagined a job. You didn't imagine millions, you imagined a minimum wage/salary. Consciousness is always objectifying itself, it is done unto you as you believe. Believing is seeing. What you can see with the physical eye is limited, what you can envision is unlimited, defined by access and exposure. I AM forever grateful. I can and will attract all things through my imagination (spiritual mind) that strengthens and guides me, by saying "YES" to life, living my intention, planting some beauty every day, and counting all costs. I AM, one creator (the individual authority over my life and decisions), one Soul (the individualized consciousness of source energy), made from one blood, one flesh, one spirit. I AM at ONE I and my creator. (SOURCE) are one. All is one. the Way of Consciousness

(…)

All is energy, all is god (SOURCE), all is one. And all energy is attracted to like energy. Yes, energy is attracted to like energy. The more energy that is collected in one area the more attraction there is. The best example of this is gravity from planetary bodies. Center yourself on your desire, it creates the gravitational pull. Your energy vibrations attract like energy to you. This means whatever is a similar vibration to you will appear in your life. There are no coincidences. You have that life energy working in you. It's the movement of the life that attracts similar life in the form of people, situations, events and the different experiences of life. Life is no fluke and gives you

8

what you actually savor in your heart. It's about what kind of intent you hold inside. Thoughts are also energy. Move your thoughts in a bounded territory, with definite paths and patterns. I AM forever grateful. I can and will attract all things through my imagination (spiritual mind) that strengthens and guides me, by saying "YES" to life, living my intention, planting some beauty every day, and counting all costs. I AM, one creator (the individual authority over my life and decisions), one Soul (the individualized consciousness of source energy), made from one blood, one flesh, one spirit. I AM at ONE I and my creator. (SOURCE) are one. All is one. the Way of Consciousness

(…)

Everything on the planet outside of nature, has come out of the human imagination. Stop and think about that for a moment. All that has manifested into reality is a projection of the inner world of the human imagination. That is why it is said that the kingdom of heaven is within, all that one desires to be, to do, and to have comes from within. The imaginative man/woman does not deny this reality. Become conscious of this reality and one no longer needs a king, a master but realizes the inner activity of divine consciousness. The inner world is the inspiration for all we see in manifested reality. The human imagination is your savior, discover the genie in the bottle. I AM forever grateful. I can and will attract all things through my imagination (spiritual mind) that strengthens and guides me, by saying "YES" to life, living my intention, planting some beauty every day, and counting all costs. I AM, one creator (the individual authority over my life and decisions), one Soul (the individualized consciousness of source energy), made from one blood, one flesh, one spirit. I AM at ONE I and my creator. (SOURCE) are one. All is one. the Way of Consciousness

(…)

What drives us to see an enemy? All that we encounter is part of ourselves. All is one. Ignorance is our only enemy. The

unconscious man/woman's blindness heeds to the undesirable expressions of life, always fighting to be free of what might come in the future. Freedom is always in the present tense. Instead of fighting against the future, claim to be that which you desire to be. All experiences follow that in which you stake claim to. I AM completely free, and I can better comprehend/ understand my brother's and sister's ignorance in their journey is the blindness to overcome or not. All will be shaken to be awakened. We are eye witnessing to the process of evolving. I see the infinite source continually awakening the planet, people, I don't have to. I must pay attention to my inner conflict that I may be further awakened, it all overlaps. It is a continual awakening, the process of evolving. I AM forever grateful. I can and will attract all things through my imagination (spiritual mind) that strengthens and guides me, by saying "YES" to life, living my intention, planting some beauty every day, and counting all costs. I AM, one creator (the individual authority over my life and decisions), one Soul (the individualized consciousness of source energy), made from one blood, one flesh, one spirit. I AM at ONE I and my creator. (SOURCE) are one. All is one.
the Way of Consciousness

(...)

To evolve is to develop gradually. Life will give you what is most helpful for your evolution. The human creature has been developing from an embryo since its conception and never stops. From the shock of breathing the first breath, to falling down learning to walk, to the blood loss involved in pulling the first set of teeth, to the trials of new acquaintances/friendship, to accepting rejection. The human journey is one of pain/pleasure/growth and evolving. And then some get to a point where pain and growth is halted, no longer wanted because of a belief that it stops at a particular age, set of circumstances, or at a belief in some kind of salvation. Awakening/evolving is not a destination it is a journey. When you are of the belief that evolving should cease, death takes command of the journey. Death knocks when there are no more

10

lessons to learn, time to become fertilizer for other growth. I will continue to transform the restrictions of a conservative reality as I evolve. I AM forever grateful. I can and will attract all things through my imagination (spiritual mind) that strengthens and guides me, by saying "YES" to life, living my intention, planting some beauty every day, and counting all costs. I AM, one creator (the individual authority over my life and decisions), one Soul (the individualized consciousness of source energy), made from one blood, one flesh, one spirit. I AM at ONE I and my creator. (SOURCE) are one. All is one. the Way of Consciousness

(…)

Responding to negativity is never about the negative energy we are being confronted with. It always has been and always will be about the energy we respond with. The kind of energy we put out is always about what we are planting. It is about what we are expressing at any given moment. It is about you and your harvest regardless of the circumstances. It is how the game goes. Nothing happens in a vacuum, your position in life has a recurring history. The harvest/circumstances came out of what was planted yesterday. Most religions believe sin/negativity is about what Adam did, but for those I say what about what you did? To pay the cost, first comes with accepting responsibility for our actions. Count all costs, the just and the unjust actions we commit. I AM forever grateful. I can and will attract all things through my imagination (spiritual mind) that strengthens and guides me, by saying "YES" to life, living my intention, planting some beauty every day, and counting all costs. I AM, one creator (the individual authority over my life and decisions), one Soul (the individualized consciousness of source energy), made from one blood, one flesh, one spirit. I AM at ONE I and my creator. (SOURCE) are one. All is one. the Way of Consciousness

(…)

Healing is the process of the restoration of health from unbalanced, diseased, damaged or unvitalized organism.

Healing is to make sound or whole, free from sickness, or injury. To restore to original purity or integrity, to overcome, to mend. The average healing time for a broken bone is 6-8 weeks. Total healing for a laceration can take days, months, or even years. It may take a few years for internal organs to heal after surgery. What about the mental healing from a broken heart? Healing does not take place in the time frame of a 30-minute sitcom. However, your arteries regenerate themselves, a few areas of the brain, your intestines, your skin and even your lungs. All you need to do is create the ideal conditions, support the whole process and maintain a healthy lifestyle that doesn't further contribute to the damage done to those organs. In other words, don't aggravate the healing process. "It is done unto you as you believe." By the law of reversibility your subconscious must objectify that which it affirms. Affirm and let the healing take its natural course. I AM forever grateful. I can and will attract all things through my imagination (spiritual mind) that strengthens and guides me, by saying "YES" to life, living my intention, planting some beauty every day, and counting all costs. I AM, one creator (the individual authority over my life and decisions), one Soul (the individualized consciousness of source energy), made from one blood, one flesh, one spirit. I AM at ONE I and my creator. (SOURCE) are one. All is one. the Way of Consciousness

(…)

"Two shall agree on touching anything and I shall establish it on earth" The two things that touch and agree are what it is your desire and working towards it. Both your desire from the conscious mind which you impregnate into the subconscious mind through focus and practice are the two that touch in your awareness of being, doing and having. Manifestation is when the agreement has been attained. I have attained that in which I desired through the consciousness of already claiming that in which I am conscious of being, doing, and having. The mystical union of your desire and your efforts are consummated giving birth to that in which you are conscious of. The world of expressions confirms this union. The moment there is a

12

touching between the conscious and subconscious minds an offspring appears. The true union/marriage can only be made in heaven (the mind) and can only be dissolved in heaven (the mind). I AM forever grateful. I can and will attract all things through my imagination (spiritual mind) that strengthens and guides me, by saying "YES" to life, living my intention, planting some beauty every day, and counting all costs. I AM, one creator (the individual authority over my life and decisions), one Soul (the individualized consciousness of source energy), made from one blood, one flesh, one spirit. I AM at ONE I and my creator. (SOURCE) are one. All is one. the Way of Consciousness

(…)

How can you explain what cannot be explained to everyone at the same time? The Bible uses symbolic persons, places, and things to articulate the thoughts and revelations of mind expressed in language. It is all symbolic language that contradicts itself if taken literally. How can you be saved if salvation is to come? Salvation, the kingdom of heaven is here. It can't be here and coming at the same time. Can your desire save you from whatever problem you have if realized? Problems seek through desire the solution, which is always knocking at the door. Desire comes from the imagination. First mother uses her imagination to keep us safe from all hurt, harm, and danger, then individual awareness and the use of our own god given imagination saves us. Get a dream, a desire, a vision, and walk it out. I AM forever grateful. I can and will attract all things through my imagination (spiritual mind) that strengthens and guides me, by saying "YES" to life, living my intention, planting some beauty every day, and counting all costs. I AM, one creator (the individual authority over my life and decisions), one Soul (the individualized consciousness of source energy), made from one blood, one flesh, one spirit. I AM at ONE I and my creator. (SOURCE) are one. All is one. the Way of Consciousness

(…)

It is not what we know that can bring us to harm's way because we can navigate that in which we know. It is not what we don't know that bring us into harm's way because we can study and prepare and navigate for what we know that we don't know. It is what we don't know that we don't know that is the challenge. How can you know what you don't know that you don't know? What we become/destiny is fashioned out of what we are not conscious of. Be conscious of what you plant." I of myself can do nothing, the Father within (the subconscious mind) doeth the work." It is unknown what happens in the germination process, how the subconscious mind doeth the work, however the harvest will be plentiful. Don't plant to impress, plant to express beauty, love, and truth and it will be your harvest. I AM forever grateful. I can and will attract all things through my imagination (spiritual mind) that strengthens and guides me, by saying "YES" to life, living my intention, planting some beauty every day, and counting all costs. I AM, one creator (the individual authority over my life and decisions), one Soul (the individualized consciousness of source energy), made from one blood, one flesh, one spirit. I AM at ONE I and my creator. (SOURCE) are one. All is one.

the Way of Consciousness

(...)

The mind/imagination, consciousness is the birth of all expression. Think back to when you were just a babe. What did you express? Now that your conscious mind has been fed through your environment/culture what do you now express? Yes, you get to express what you have been fed. Impressions create expressions! Consciousness of the thing to be desired precedes the expression/manifestation of whatever it is we desire to be /to do or to have. Expression is always preceded by the conscious awareness of that to be expressed. Create your masterpiece through your own mental diet. The impressions are impregnated into the subconscious mind, when accepted over time become expressions of that visualized into that which is materialized. I AM forever grateful. I can and will attract all things through my imagination (spiritual mind) that

14

strengthens and guides me, by saying "YES" to life, living my intention, planting some beauty every day, and counting all costs. I AM, one creator (the individual authority over my life and decisions), one Soul (the individualized consciousness of source energy), made from one blood, one flesh, one spirit. I AM at ONE I and my creator. (SOURCE) are one. All is one. the Way of Consciousness

(…)

Can you see my home training, the image that I represent, what I bear witness to? The apple does not fall far from the tree. You say you have been born again, however how can your conception of yourself be less than that which conceived you (god/SOURCE)? As it is understood after the rebirth the I AM, FATHER, your consciousness is recognized as the indwelling spirit of the "MOST HIGH'. The "MOST HIGH" is one consciousness. When man/woman observes the law of one consciousness she/he will understand I and my father/SOURCE are one. The conceiver and the conception are one. All is one. Say what you will, but actions speak louder than words. In your actions you are defining that which conceived you. Your actions will define what you have named god/SOURCE of that which you have become. It is evident what you bear witness to without opening your mouth. "Go into all the world and spread love/the gospel, and use words when absolutely necessary," St. Francis. The son, that which is conceived bears witness of the father/the conceiver. Bear witness! I AM forever grateful. I can and will attract all things through my imagination (spiritual mind) that strengthens and guides me, by saying "YES" to life, living my intention, planting some beauty every day, and counting all costs. I AM, one creator (the individual authority over my life and decisions), one Soul (the individualized consciousness of source energy), made from one blood, one flesh, one spirit. I AM at ONE I and my creator. (SOURCE) are one. All is one. the Way of Consciousness

(…)

I don't want to go back. I remember what was back there and why I wanted to move forward. To go back is to return to a former or less developed state. Talk over again. To join, or return to, a group, place or position again (date from/back to). To originate a particular time, having existed since. Not to conceptualize anew, afresh, or to develop a replacement concept of. I AM looking ahead as a child seeking that which lies ahead. I AM forever grateful. I can and will attract all things through my imagination (spiritual mind) that strengthens and guides me, by saying "YES" to life, living my intention, planting some beauty every day, and counting all costs. I AM, one creator (the individual authority over my life and decisions), one Soul (the individualized consciousness of source energy), made from one blood, one flesh, one spirit. I AM at ONE I and my creator. (SOURCE) are one. All is one. the Way of Consciousness

(…)

How can heaven be at hand, here and now, and also be a place we go to when we die? Heaven/the divine mind is everywhere present. It is a frequency that allows the creation of stuff. "The kingdom of heaven cometh not with observation; neither say, Lo here! Or there for lo, the kingdom of god is within you." Heaven is a state of consciousness in which the soul and the body are in harmony with the Divine Mind. All is mind. Tune in. Woman/man adjust their thought world to the kingdom of divine ideas through a process of denial by which he/she eliminates from consciousness all inharmonious ideas, and through affirmations of truth by which he/he establishes him/herself in harmony with such ideas. It is feeling the majesty of it all, the earth, life and all the stuff we can't explain. Seek, find what gives you joy and go there. I AM forever grateful. I can and will attract all things through my imagination (spiritual mind) that strengthens and guides me, by saying "YES" to life, living my intention, planting some beauty every day, and counting all costs. I AM, one creator (the individual authority over my life and decisions), one Soul (the individualized consciousness of source energy), made from one

16

blood, one flesh, one spirit. I AM at ONE I and my creator. (SOURCE) are one. All is one.
the Way of Consciousness

(…)

The conscious mind reasons inductively and the subconscious mind reasons deductively. Inductive reasoning makes observations and relates them to your previous experiences, and education. It makes it difficult to believe what the senses deny. Once the senses deny a thing, it becomes a miracle, or magic with realization. Deductive reasoning is the process of drawing a conclusion based on premises that are generally assumed to be true. That is why "It is done unto you as you believe." The subconscious mind will operate out of what you believe to be true, whether it is factual or not. Faith/imagination in unseen reality gives expression based on the premise set forth through one's acceptance. This means regardless of your circumstances, if you can dream it, you can be it. You can do it. Miracles and magic become the norm, the ordinary. "Just do it." I AM forever grateful. I can and will attract all things through my imagination (spiritual mind) that strengthens and guides me, by saying "YES" to life, living my intention, planting some beauty every day, and counting all costs. I AM, one creator (the individual authority over my life and decisions), one Soul (the individualized consciousness of source energy), made from one blood, one flesh, one spirit. I AM at ONE I and my creator. (SOURCE) are one. All is one.
the Way of Consciousness

(…)

Reality is created, the means are manifested by the acceptance of an idea. Imagination starts the process. Belief in the thing hoped for carries it through the gestation process. And finally, we give birth to that which was once just an idea. Without faith, a continuous belief in the thing hoped for (the son), the thing hoped for will miscarry. "Not by might, nor by power, "but faith in the desired outcome, dedication to purpose, discipline, and focus, attract what you believe to be true. Sounds simple

enough. I AM forever grateful. I can and will attract all things through my imagination (spiritual mind) that strengthens and guides me, by saying "YES" to life, living my intention, planting some beauty every day, and counting all costs. I AM, one creator (the individual authority over my life and decisions), one Soul (the individualized consciousness of source energy), made from one blood, one flesh, one spirit. I AM at ONE I and my creator. (SOURCE) are one. All is one.
the Way of Consciousness

(...)

The Divine Mind is a tangible living Light that gives shape to creation. It's the eternal thought of God within that possesses all the divine potentials we will ever experience. To reach its potential, the human mind feeds at all times. Even when you sleep the mind feeds, dreams appear. Have a definite mental diet or the mind will wonder into the course of observed events. The universe does not align with "I will". The universe joins in and adheres to I AM. Be definite. Actualize fully the imagination and think from the end of your ideas instead of thinking of the end. "Let the weak man say I AM strong." Imagine how life will appear if you have accomplished that in which you desire, if you are strong. As vibrational beings it is necessary to occupy the frequency of life fulfilled to achieve fulfillment, be. I AM forever grateful. I can and will attract all things through my imagination (spiritual mind) that strengthens and guides me, by saying "YES" to life, living my intention, planting some beauty every day, and counting all costs. I AM, one creator (the individual authority over my life and decisions), one Soul (the individualized consciousness of source energy), made from one blood, one flesh, one spirit. I AM at ONE I and my creator. (SOURCE) are one. All is one.
the Way of Consciousness

(...)

Who are you beyond your historical life situation? There is but one Mind, and that Mind cannot be separated or divided, because, like the principle of mathematics, it is indivisible. All
18

that we can say of the one Mind is that it is absolute and that all of its manifestations are in essence like itself. You are a microorganism of the macro-organism. The Divine Mind is like the ocean, you a pond, and your cells a droplet of water. All is one. And all operate in unison with directed focus. Our conscious processing capacity is significant, but clearly, it's just a retention pond compared to the ocean of total mind/consciousness. Not by power, not by might but by focus, all things come to pass from thought to expression. I AM forever grateful. I can and will attract all things through my imagination (spiritual mind) that strengthens and guides me, by saying "YES" to life, living my intention, planting some beauty every day, and counting all costs. I AM, one creator (the individual authority over my life and decisions), one Soul (the individualized consciousness of source energy), made from one blood, one flesh, one spirit. I AM at ONE I and my creator. (SOURCE) are one. All is one.
the Way of Consciousness

(…)

What does it mean to think and live from the end? All that has been and will be created is the result of what enters the mind. Imagine life from that place in which your dream has been fulfilled. Imagine what you would be doing if all your dreams and desires have come to pass and start living as if it is so. When you imagine watching a movie, you first imagine what is you want to see. You turn the TV on, go to the channel, and your desire appears just as you believed it to be so. It's the same with preparing a meal. You imagine being fulfilled in the process of cooking. When going on a trip, you pack what you are going to wear before you get there and imagine turning heads, etc. This is the fundamental use of imagination to achieve desires. Go for it! I AM forever grateful. I can and will attract all things through my imagination (spiritual mind) that strengthens and guides me, by saying "YES" to life, living my intention, planting some beauty every day, and counting all costs. I AM, one creator (the individual authority over my life and decisions), one Soul (the individualized consciousness of

19

source energy), made from one blood, one flesh, one spirit. I AM at ONE I and my creator. (SOURCE) are one. All is one. the Way of Consciousness

(...)

Everyone has two eyes, but no one has the same view. There can be no substitute for our own experiences. The outward ceremonies we partake in cannot take us to inner truth. There is an inner commitment/observation involved in all we discover. Our hope lies in our own realization of that which lies within us. Only I can express my feelings. What I see and allowed to be is a direct reflection of what I feel, my state of consciousness. What do you see unfolding with the new day? Believing is seeing. I AM forever grateful. I can and will attract all things through my imagination (spiritual mind) that strengthens and guides me, by saying "YES" to life, living my intention, planting some beauty every day, and counting all costs. I AM, one creator (the individual authority over my life and decisions), one Soul (the individualized consciousness of source energy), made from one blood, one flesh, one spirit. I AM at ONE I and my creator. (SOURCE) are one. All is one. the Way of Consciousness

(...)

The reason prayer works is because it is an expression of thought, a thought that you hold. In the beginning was the word. And a word is an expression of thought. Words can give you the energy and motivation to start taking charge in life and will give you more control over yourself and your choices. Everything begins and ends with a thought, a choice. The only way to change your condition is to change your mind. Change your mind. Change your reality. So, you say you are waiting on a savior to return to make all things right with the world. As you have seen from history, either the savior has to hold your mind or you will revert back to who your mind says you are. Because of free will, in the allegory, the infinite did not hold Adam's mind when he was tempted, so what makes you think you will be able to hold yours upon your saviors return? Adam and Eve

20

lived under the reign of no mind, bliss. It didn't work. Allow your imagination to be your savior and hold the thoughts that bring you joy. I AM forever grateful. I can and will attract all things through my imagination (spiritual mind) that strengthens and guides me, by saying "YES" to life, living my intention, planting some beauty every day, and counting all costs. I AM, one creator (the individual authority over my life and decisions), one Soul (the individualized consciousness of source energy), made from one blood, one flesh, one spirit. I AM at ONE I and my creator. (SOURCE) are one. All is one. the Way of Consciousness

(...)

Chance is a dangerous or uncertain outcome, the unpredictable and uncontrollable element of an occurrence. Choice is an act of selecting or making a decision when faced with two or more possibilities, a preferred destination. A choice without a plan is just a wish/chance. Live under choice not a chance. Every single thing you do; you are choosing a direction. The direction of our lives comes down to the choices we make. If you don't like your life, it's time to make better choices. The choice is yours. I can and will do all things through my imagination (mind) that strengthens and guides me, by saying no to everything else, counting all costs. I AM forever grateful. I can and will attract all things through my imagination (spiritual mind) that strengthens and guides me, by saying "YES" to life, living my intention, planting some beauty every day, and counting all costs. I AM, one creator (the individual authority over my life and decisions), one Soul (the individualized consciousness of source energy), made from one blood, one flesh, one spirit. I AM at ONE I and my creator. (SOURCE) are one. All is one. the Way of Consciousness

(...)

We do not love people because of who they are but because of who we are. We've all been wronged at some point in our lives. It hurts and we all understand how that feels. When you respond with love you don't put yourself in the position to have to say

I'm sorry. But if you do respond out of a temporary negative character, remember forgiveness is not about what the other person or party did or didn't do but your response to their actions. The most frustrating fact about holding on to the hurt and not forgiving is that you're giving up your power to lead a happy existence. The pain and anger you hold towards any person who offended you means that he or she has control over your thoughts and feelings. If you really want the last word, APOLOGIZE. Forgiving is your way to make right your actions. It allows you to be at peace while holding a grudge only fills the heart with bitterness. I forgive because I want to be forgiven when my time comes. Forgiveness sets you free. I AM forever grateful. I can and will attract all things through my imagination (spiritual mind) that strengthens and guides me, by saying "YES" to life, living my intention, planting some beauty every day, and counting all costs. I AM, one creator (the individual authority over my life and decisions), one Soul (the individualized consciousness of source energy), made from one blood, one flesh, one spirit. I AM at ONE I and my creator. (SOURCE) are one. All is one.
the Way of Consciousness

(…)

Psalms 82:6 "I have said, **Ye are gods**; and all of you are children of the Most High." King James Version (**KJV**) John 10:34 "Jesus answered them, it is written in your law, I said, Ye are Gods." Man/Woman are the gods of their reality. All we see outside of nature has come out of the divine mind of man/woman. What idea has been fulfilled out of your mind? The unconscious processing abilities of the mind are estimated at roughly 11 million pieces of information per second. In addition, research is uncovering abilities of this unconscious processing abilities to defy reason. This ability within us, imagination operates more effective when man/woman remembers that we are divine beings. Imagine from your divine nature, not your human nature. I AM forever grateful. I can and will attract all things through my imagination (spiritual mind) that strengthens and guides me, by saying "YES" to life,

22

living my intention, planting some beauty every day, and counting all costs. I AM, one creator (the individual authority over my life and decisions), one Soul (the individualized consciousness of source energy), made from one blood, one flesh, one spirit. I AM at ONE I and my creator. (SOURCE) are one. All is one.

the Way of Consciousness

(…)

Expression comes from within and gives life to that which has only been imagined. Expression is an act, a process, or instance of manifesting, bringing to life one's thoughts and feelings. Expression moves reality/everything from the invisible to the visible realm. Putting pen to paper is the writer's way of expression. The pen is the tool that gives life, brings to paper that which has been imagined. Again, given a canvas and paint, the painter's brush is the tool that creates the magic. All human creativity comes forth out of the human imagination. As co-creators, that which we have imagined is also brought forth with a tool design specifically for our supernatural abilities. That tool when used intentionally will bring forth all the desires of your heart. That tool, which is your deliverer, your magic wand/genie in the bottle is FOCUS. It brings what you have imagined to earth. The scriptures use parables that show FOCUS within the context of individual persistent effort/fortitude, and forthrightness. Forge ahead. Everything that you have ever imaged in life came/comes forth with FOCUS. Don't lose faith, don't give up and don't look back, take full responsibility for the incarnation of your desires with FOCUS in hand. I AM forever grateful. I can and will attract all things through my imagination (spiritual mind) that strengthens and guides me, by saying "YES" to life, living my intention, planting some beauty every day, and counting all costs. I AM, one creator (the individual authority over my life and decisions), one Soul (the individualized consciousness of source energy), made from one blood, one flesh, one spirit. I AM at ONE I and my creator. (SOURCE) are one. All is one.

(…)

What is your goal? In other words, what is the object of your ambition or effort? What is the target/ aim or desired result of your life on earth? Is it to help yourself, help people, get money or maybe just to make the world a better place one day and one person/encounter at a time? Your goal will manifest your actions. And your actions consist of believing it is already done. The feeling for the wish fulfilled is a necessary condition of man's/woman's search for the goal. The stop light doesn't mean the light is not going to change. It only means that it's someone else's time to move forward or maybe just to slow your roll. I AM forever grateful. I can and will attract all things through my imagination (spiritual mind) that strengthens and guides me, by saying "YES" to life, living my intention, planting some beauty every day, and counting all costs. I AM, one creator (the individual authority over my life and decisions), one Soul (the individualized consciousness of source energy), made from one blood, one flesh, one spirit. I AM at ONE I and my creator. (SOURCE) are one. All is one.

(…)

An ideology is a comprehensive vision, a way of looking at things that respond with tendencies, or a set of ideas proposed by the dominant class of a society to all members of this society. An ideology is a set of conscious and unconscious ideas that constitute one's goals, expectations, and actions towards you. So, do you believe in symbolism and ideology? What does your life symbolize? What is the ideology of white supremacy, black power, a woman's place, children should be seen and not heard? Ideology is a problem because it leads to closed-mindedness, motivated reasoning and self-righteousness. It tends to stop skeptical inquiry and genuine discourse. As soon as you look at the world through an ideology you are finished. No reality fits an ideology. Use the same thought process of love, of wonder and of acceptance you had when you came out of your mother's womb. I AM forever grateful. I can and will attract all things through my imagination (spiritual mind) that strengthens and guides me, by saying "YES" to life, living my intention, planting some beauty every day, and counting all costs. I AM, one creator (the individual authority over my life and decisions), one Soul (the individualized consciousness of source energy), made from one blood, one flesh, one spirit. I AM at ONE I and my creator. (SOURCE) are one. All is one. the Way of Consciousness

(…)

Love for lack of a better word is the highest Frequency of positive energy. So, the goal is to think Love. How can I think love in this encounter? How can I think love consistently with each encounter? Think love, it is not rehearsed, it is not a benevolent act, it is a feeling, it will show me what to do. Giving a "cup of water" is the way the scriptures explain it. The "cup of water" is your psychological truth that will save the situation and carry it as an expression of love. Then to live that truth is to turn the water into wine. Imagine what I must do to save myself from the present situation. Give a "cup of water" shows compassion, shows love from your sense of expressiveness. Without an imagination expressing the power within you will need an outside savior because of your lack of understanding this truth. I AM forever grateful. I can and will attract all things through my imagination (spiritual mind) that strengthens and guides me, by saying "YES" to life, living my intention, planting some beauty every day, and counting all costs. I AM, one creator (the individual authority over my life and decisions), one Soul (the individualized consciousness of source energy), made from one blood, one flesh, one spirit. I AM at ONE I and my creator. (SOURCE) are one. All is one. the Way of Consciousness

(…)

Where opportunities are seized, they multiply. You are a multiplier. The factor by which the return deriving from an expenditure exceeds the expenditure itself. A means increasing

by repetition and intensity to force a measurable level. You are one that creates abundance. You derived from god, a derivative of god. "**Let us make man in our image**, after **our** likeness" and god multiplies god self through the human race. Can you count the leaves on the trees, the stars in the sky? Everything on the planet is in abundance. Ever been to a buffet? "And you, be ye fruitful, and **multiply**; bring **forth** abundantly in the earth, and **multiply** therein." Who told you this scripture was about bearing children? So, take the talent from him who did not multiply not one and give it to him who has the ten talents. For to everyone who has will more be given, and he will have an abundance. "When he got to the tree, there was nothing but fig leaves. He said, "No more figs from this tree—ever!" The fig tree withered on the spot, a dry stick. Multiply something, anything and bring forth an abundance. Yourself, or a product, and you will be rewarded abundantly. I AM forever grateful. I can and will attract all things through my imagination (spiritual mind) that strengthens and guides me, by saying "YES" to life, living my intention, planting some beauty every day, and counting all costs. I AM, one creator (the individual authority over my life and decisions), one Soul (the individualized consciousness of source energy), made from one blood, one flesh, one spirit. I AM at ONE I and my creator. (SOURCE) are one. All is one.
the Way of Consciousness

(…)

Derivative; formed from another. The infinite/god is the sum/total of all of its parts. Everything is. I AM, a derivative of God/SOURCE. God/SOURCE only exist because of me, my perception and I only exist because of god/SOURCE. Without my personal perception god/SOURCE would not exist within me. And without God/SOURCE my personal perception would not exist. I and my father/god/SOURCE are one. I have to view, perceive god/SOURCE in a way that empowers me. I AM forever grateful. I can and will attract all things through my imagination (spiritual mind) that strengthens and guides me, by saying "YES" to life, living my

26

intention, planting some beauty every day, and counting all costs. I AM, one creator (the individual authority over my life and decisions), one Soul (the individualized consciousness of source energy), made from one blood, one flesh, one spirit. I AM at ONE I and my creator. (SOURCE) are one. All is one. the Way of Consciousness

(...)

"The meek shall inherit the earth." Why? Because the universe is ever evolving and those with a current leg up can become prideful and resentful of new technology/ideas. Meek is defined as patient, without resentment; not willing to argue or express opinions in a forceful way; modest; not arrogant or prideful. The spirit mind (Moses) follows what we cannot see, the invisible reality (imagination). The carnal mind follows what can be seen (Aaron), what someone else has imagined for you. And the people said, "Give us what we can see." (programming). However, we can learn from any paradigm and see why the meek shall inherit the earth." In the evolution of the transportation model: the horse, the carriage, the horse and buggy were imagined means of transportation that came to life. The benefactors became arrogant, prideful with wealth, and eventually lost it all. Then the stagecoach carried more people longer distances. The benefactors became arrogant, prideful with wealth, and eventually lost it all. What goes up must come down. Next came the train: capable of caring more people longer distances, and a lot faster. Recent technology has brought forth the fuel powered automobile, the boat, the helicopter, the airplane, the spaceship...You get the picture. The universe is constantly expanding, and you want to be a conservative? Good luck! The meek shall inherit the earth because today's monopoly will evolve into something else, know that. Follow what you cannot see, imagination, the spiritual mind (Moses)/imagination. I AM forever grateful. I can and will attract all things through my imagination (spiritual mind) that strengthens and guides me, by saying "YES" to life, living my intention, planting some beauty every day, and counting all costs. I AM, one creator (the individual authority over my life and decisions), one Soul (the individualized consciousness of source energy), made from one blood, one flesh, one spirit. I AM at ONE I and my creator. (SOURCE) are one. All is one.

the Way of Consciousness

(...)

To desire/want your soul to go to heaven, wouldn't you first have to understand what your soul is and how it works? In many religious, philosophical, and mythological traditions, the soul is the incorporeal essence of a living being (god likeness/ invisible image). It is the eternal you. It existed with the stars (star child) and will return to the stars (eternity). The soul has no gender, race or creed. Neither Jew nor Greek, black or white. All religions and prophets are trying to teach you how to be a soul with an Avatar body within the earthly realm of consciousness. The soul is hidden beneath the flesh. Judge not because the soul doesn't judge. It is not a respecter of person and lives at the highest frequency/ love. The soul gives to the just and the unjust. Ptah in the Kemet and also Greek philosophers, such as Socrates, Plato, and Aristotle, understood that the soul must have a logical faculty, the exercise of which is the most divine of human actions. The kingdom of heaven is at hand/ the rebirth of the soul simply means I have had enough of fleshly living and begins to allow the soul run the show. This is the way, the path. Soul work is the process of bringing the essential self - the soul - out of hiding. It's a fundamental shift away from occupying the constructed self (flesh), and towards the art of living from our soul/the god self. Allow your essence /soul to move us towards wholeness. I AM forever grateful. I can and will attract all things through my imagination (spiritual mind) that strengthens and guides me, by saying "YES" to life, living my intention, planting some beauty every day, and counting all costs. I AM, one creator (the individual authority over my life and decisions), one Soul (the individualized consciousness of source energy), made from one blood, one

28

flesh, one spirit. I AM at ONE I and my creator. (SOURCE) are one. All is one.

the Way of Consciousness

(…)

How do you expect the universe to support your life's choice/path and you haven't chosen one? If your child acknowledged that he/she wanted to be a baseball player and you wanted to support their aspirations, what would you provide for them in their pursuit of their goal? A glove, a bat, maybe the full gear, and an opportunity to get in a game somewhere. It would apply to any goal: football, tennis, or a music career. The kingdom of heaven is reached when one understands who he/she is and what he/she stands for. At that point things can be added. Until then what is the universe adding to? Once you find the thing that motivates you regardless of prior and future circumstances, you are there. It is your theme/purpose/path/motivator. Once found, and you're on solid ground, unwavering, the subconscious mind will do what it does as a magnet and draw all consistent things unto thee. Yes, it's faith but it is also quantum physics. Like attracts like, consistency comes with a chosen direction, focus kicks in, thine eye becomes single, and manifestation occurs. If you are bonded over money, lust, hate, drugs, or strife, know what comes with that. You will have to stay that way to stay bonded. It's not based on right and wrong but direction. I AM forever grateful. I can and will attract all things through my imagination (spiritual mind) that strengthens and guides me, by saying "YES" to life, living my intention, planting some beauty every day, and counting all costs. I AM, one creator (the individual authority over my life and decisions), one Soul (the individualized consciousness of source energy), made from one blood, one flesh, one spirit. I AM at ONE I and my creator. (SOURCE) are one. All is one.

the Way of Consciousness

(…)

Where does reality come from? Reality leaves everything to the imagination. It's how things work in the tangible world of shape and form. And it is your belief which brings forth the reality you experience. If your mind is the hardware, then your **beliefs are** the software. It is the operating system that gathers, stores and manages information based on how you perceive yourself and your life. Your belief is that which the mind uses to create the role you assume. Our views and perceptions of the world determine what we can and cannot have, what we will and will not achieve and determines what is possible or not possible. There is NO aspect of life that is immune to the fact that perception is reality and determines the kind and quality of our reality individually. If we want to change the reality, ultimately, we have to change the way we think, feel and perceive. I AM forever grateful. I can and will attract all things through my imagination (spiritual mind) that strengthens and guides me, by saying "YES" to life, living my intention, planting some beauty every day, and counting all costs. I AM, one creator (the individual authority over my life and decisions), one Soul (the individualized consciousness of source energy), made from one blood, one flesh, one spirit. I AM at ONE I and my creator. (SOURCE) are one. All is one.
the Way of Consciousness

(…)

One of the purposes of education is to expose/familiarize the student learner to what the environment consists of. There is limited exposure consisting of general education in K through 12th grade and it gets more specific as it expands. Everything expands/vibrates, nothing is at rest. And everything has to be maintained in order that expansion doesn't outgrow the consistency of stability. That is one of the jobs of government on the macro level, to maintain the "consistency of stability." For those that understand home maintenance and construction or just live somewhere this lesson will assist in understanding the supply/SOURCE. Everything has a beginning from the invisible realm including you. Let's say a window needs to be replaced and you go to a specific retailer. Now that can be

30

Anderson Windows, Pella Windows, Lowes, Window Word, etc. The same manufacturer makes all the retail windows and distributes to each retailer with their particular logo. People are buying the brand/logo, because of who stands behind it, however all the windows come from one manufacturer. The product is assembled, branded and shipped. It is the same product with different variations and logos. It is the same with religion, each retailor/denomination charges for their brand/logo, however the manufacturer/creator, it is available to all who want pay the wholesale price for distribution rights. For a better deal, I say skip the middleman and go straight to the manufacturer/SOURCE. I AM forever grateful. I can and will attract all things through my imagination (spiritual mind) that strengthens and guides me, by saying "YES" to life, living my intention, planting some beauty every day, and counting all costs. I AM, one creator (the individual authority over my life and decisions), one Soul (the individualized consciousness of source energy), made from one blood, one flesh, one spirit. I AM at ONE I and my creator. (SOURCE) are one. All is one. the Way of Consciousness

(…)

The mind/flesh is unwilling to admit that god subjects god's self to god's law. Do you desire understanding, over standing, or inner standing? Everything comes from the invisible/inner standing. The inner standing/the invisible is built on natural law. What do you stand on? It is god's pleasure to give you whatever you desire. The great secret is controlled imagination and sustained attention. It all comes from inner standing. The soul is the mystical union between you (the derivative) and god (the sum/total of everything). The soul operates by believing what you are feeling. It brings you more of what you are feeling based on the notion that your feeling is that which you long for. It makes what is imagined and felt real. Because it is the god's presence in you, the soul does not eat of the tree of knowledge of good and evil. It is not man/flesh. It is the higher self, the god self, it contains and maintains the attributes of god. We have the power to imagine and create whatever we affirm. It is the

31

law of the land. Our superpower is focus and we are only limited by weakness of attention and poverty of imagination. Life gives you whatever you focus on. Stay in tune with that which is to be accomplished. I AM forever grateful. I can and will attract all things through my imagination (spiritual mind) that strengthens and guides me, by saying "YES" to life, living my intention, planting some beauty every day, and counting all costs. I AM, one creator (the individual authority over my life and decisions), one Soul (the individualized consciousness of source energy), made from one blood, one flesh, one spirit. I AM at ONE I and my creator. (SOURCE) are one. All is one.

the Way of Consciousness

(…)

When someone tells you to use your mind, who are they talking to? If you have to be trained to use your mind, then the mind is not you. The soul is you, however it is beyond you. God/SOURCE is spirit and the soul is the singular from of spirit. The soul is the abundance of the universe in flesh. It is the eternal god-self within you. You cannot operate out of lack and expect abundance. Abundance and lack are two conflicting thoughts. To feel lack on the inside will reflect lack on the outside. As long as man/woman looks for the cause of their expression in the hopeful anticipation of another he looks in futility. "Hope" will keep you broke. The impoverished mind needs hope. Start using your mind and stop letting your mind use you based on what someone else put in it. No manifestation comes unto me accept I draw it. If not, why would I have to believe. And why doesn't everybody draw the same thing? We must persist until we find ourselves in that place in which we ourselves have imagined. I AM forever grateful. I can and will attract all things through my imagination (spiritual mind) that strengthens and guides me, by saying "YES" to life, living my intention, planting some beauty every day, and counting all costs. I AM, one creator (the individual authority over my life and decisions), one Soul (the individualized consciousness of

source energy), made from one blood, one flesh, one spirit. I AM at ONE I and my creator. (SOURCE) are one. All is one.
the Way of Consciousness

(…)

It is time for the resurrection of you. The SOUL is the immaterial essence, animating principle, or actuating cause of an individual life. Coming to earth the SOUL sacrifices its unlimited awareness to inhabit the physical body and follows a physical path. Jesus is the story of living life through the journey of the SOUL. The soul enters earth through the womb. This inhabitation of the physical body comes with limitations. We then follow the (yellow brick road) path of enlightenment until the SOUL is free. The consciousness of the soul regains its freedom and unlimited awareness when it resurrects itself. This is the field trip to earth, to resurrect the SOUL. From spirit back to spirit. The SOUL descended from god and the liberation of the soul creates a Christ that reconnects to the god self. God is spirit and through the principle of resurrecting the spirit you begin attracting desires rather than chasing physical wants. In the allegory (screenplay) Jesus, plays the role of the SOUL going through life experiences. Life gives us all the experiences we need to enlighten our individual SOUL and regain our limitless potential. Count it all joy, never loose, win or learn. Enjoy the experience. I AM forever grateful. I AM forever grateful. I can and will attract all things through my imagination (spiritual mind) that strengthens and guides me, by saying "YES" to life, living my intention, planting some beauty every day, and counting all costs. I AM, one creator (the individual authority over my life and decisions), one Soul (the individualized consciousness of source energy), made from one blood, one flesh, one spirit. I AM at ONE I and my creator. (SOURCE) are one. All is one.
the Way of Consciousness

(…)

Which poem, literary work, movie, novel, screenplay, allegory, parable, religious text, rap, song best tells the journey of your soul? Which do you resonate with? Light vs. darkness, Jack vs. the giant, David vs. Goliath, the dragon vs. the prince, Jesus vs. the devil, Darth Vader vs. Luke Skywalker, Moses vs. Pharaoh, Dorothy vs. The wicked witch, Neo (the one) vs. The machines, clean vs. unclean, Ali vs. Frazier, The Rock vs. the Undertaker, saved vs. unsaved, us vs. them, saints vs. sinners/ straight vs. gay/woke vs. sleep/conservative vs. liberal or the chosen people vs. the rest of the world? All possibilities/outcomes have to exist for everyone to get their just do in god's world. What possibilities have to be gone in your world as if you have a world except what has been indoctrinated into your mind? It is done unto you as you believe. That's the way of the world. You reap what you sow. With the same arm you use to measure it will be measured again unto you. Don't hate the player hate the game. Your challenges are the same spirit resurrected in different flesh. Don't fight the physical, walk in consciousness, awareness, the light, faith, spirit. Within your conflict arises a soul. How can you expect a new relationship/gift if you haven't forgiven the last one? If you want the last world, apologize. I AM forever grateful. I can and will attract all things through my imagination (spiritual mind) that strengthens and guides me, by saying "YES" to life, living my intention, planting some beauty every day, and counting all costs. I AM, one creator (the individual authority over my life and decisions), one Soul (the individualized consciousness of source energy), made from one blood, one flesh, one spirit. I AM at ONE I and my creator. (SOURCE) are one. All is one. the Way of Consciousness

(…)

A state of consciousness is a demand on the infinite store house, and like the law of commerce a demand creates supply. To change the supply, you change the demand, your state of consciousness. What you desire to be, you must feel you already are. Your state of consciousness creates the conditions of life, rather than the conditions create your state of consciousness. Be the solution to your own problems. I AM forever grateful. I can and will attract all things through my

34

imagination (spiritual mind) that strengthens and guides me, by saying "YES" to life, living my intention, planting some beauty every day, and counting all costs. I AM, one creator (the individual authority over my life and decisions), one Soul (the individualized consciousness of source energy), made from one blood, one flesh, one spirit. I AM at ONE I and my creator. (SOURCE) are one. All is one.

the Way of Consciousness

(…)

Moses, the symbol of the spiritual mind insisted that god /spirit has no name. Then the son of man/flesh created names for the Great Spirit to signify/ symbolize those attributes of the infinite that you/flesh might more readily recognize those attributes of spirit for your remembrance. Symbols have become so ingrained within our cultural sphere that they carry an almost universal meaning. The son of man looks for meaning in everything around us, anything can become a symbol as long as people interpret it to mean something other than its literal definition. Who doesn't immediately associate an owl with wisdom, a dove with peace, or a red rose with romance? In the allegory, The Wizard of Oz, the cowardly lion represents courage, the tin man, the heart, the scare crow a brain and Dorothy represents resourcefulness. Dorothy's silver shoes **symbolize** the so-called "silver cord" connecting a person's physical and spiritual form. The yellow brick road **signifies** the golden path to enlightenment. In the allegory of Jesus, the soul/individualized spirit is conceived/birth in the body/flesh of man /women. The son of god/the soul hidden by flesh then resurrects from turmoil/suffering/death of the flesh and rises at Golgotha (site of crucifixion) /the skull freeing the soul from the limitations of the flesh. The third/spiritual eye opens and the son of god/resurrected soul is revealed and returns to the Father (the parable of the prodigal son). Jesus symbolizes the soul/individuated spirit that will never leave you or forsake you, closer than a brother and with god all at the same time. Learn the way. I AM forever grateful. I can and will attract all things through my imagination (spiritual mind) that strengthens and guides me, by saying "YES" to life, living my intention, planting some beauty every day, and counting all costs. I AM, one creator (the individual authority over my life and decisions), one Soul (the individualized consciousness of source energy), made from one blood, one flesh, one spirit. I AM at ONE I and my creator. (SOURCE) are one. All is one. the Way of Consciousness

(…)

Thinking is a conscious exercise. Try a little thinking every day or rest on becoming a victim of circumstances. In the beginning there was nothing. We are all the product of our patterns of thinking. Thinking is the action of using one's mind to produce thoughts. Or in other words understanding, speculation, logic, cognition, scrutiny, discerning, rationalizing, deduction, contemplation, and conceiving. I AM in form, the awareness of conceiving myself with the capacity to be whatever I imagine. By the Law of Being, I AM compelled to be and express all that I believe myself to be through thought. Thoughts are ideas. Any conception begins in the mind as a result of mental understanding, awareness, and activity. I AM forever grateful. I can and will attract all things through my imagination (spiritual mind) that strengthens and guides me, by saying "YES" to life, living my intention, planting some beauty every day, and counting all costs. I AM, one creator (the individual authority over my life and decisions), one Soul (the individualized consciousness of source energy), made from one blood, one flesh, one spirit. I AM at ONE I and my creator. (SOURCE) are one. All is one. the Way of Consciousness

(…)

All is one energy. Therefore, nothing is ever created. All new forms merely result from the changing of something that was, into something else that now is. All is manifested out of what you imagine. Cells, molecules, and atoms shift to create new forms. Form: the external shape, appearance, or configuration of an object, in contrast to the matter of which it is composed,

36

a new visible space, transformation. The universe, the invisible loves form. Why? No one knows, maybe to see the manifestation of its invisible self through you, its creation, its visible self. Look around, all around is life in one form of another. Planet earth is home of 8.7 million species. Everything is formed from the invisible realm of consciousness. Everything outside of nature is formed from human consciousness. Choose from within to be a vessel of consciousness. The Universal Law of Gender creates all forms in the physical realm. The Law of Gender, the (masculine) conscious mind impregnates the subconscious (feminine mind) and the magic begins. The subconscious mind runs on auto pilot, that is why you don't have to relearn to walk every day. The universe attracts to you what has been impregnated into the subconscious mind. When you recognize the consciousness within you, which is essential and is invisible to the eye creation begins to flow through you, you attract. Without conscious awareness within, you visualize an ideal, go through the ordeal of touching the dream without counting the cost, and then want a new deal. The process of maintaining the ideal is moving from conformist (indoctrinated child mind) to non-conformist (teenage rejection mind), to transformed non-conformist (adult, you do you and I FOCUS on me, nonjudgmental mind). I AM forever grateful. I can and will attract all things through my imagination (spiritual mind) that strengthens and guides me, by saying "YES" to life, living my intention, planting some beauty every day, and counting all costs. I AM, one creator (the individual authority over my life and decisions), one Soul (the individualized consciousness of source energy), made from one blood, one flesh, one spirit. I AM at ONE I and my creator. (SOURCE) are one. All is one.

the Way of Consciousness

(…)

Do you prefer, being married or being single? Monogamy or polygamy, having children or not having children, renting a home or owning your home? Factors that can influence the impressions you form include the context of the situation, your own personal traits, your past experiences, and sensory adaptations which are affected by a number of factors, including beliefs, values, prejudices, culture, and life experiences. Moving forward I will understand who I AM, including but not limited to my attitudes, moods, motives, self-concept, interest, my individual's pattern of thinking and finally, expectations that can distort perceptions of what i will see and what i expect to see. Knowing oneself makes it easier to see things accurately. I AM forever grateful. I can and will attract all things through my imagination (spiritual mind) that strengthens and guides me, by saying "YES" to life, living my intention, planting some beauty every day, and counting all costs. I AM, one creator (the individual authority over my life and decisions), one Soul (the individualized consciousness of source energy), made from one blood, one flesh, one spirit. I AM at ONE I and my creator. (SOURCE) are one. All is one. the Way of Consciousness

(…)

What have you been indoctrinated with by the environment? The indoctrinated mind that is conflicted will attract conflict. Clean vs. unclean, saved vs. unsaved, us vs them, I AM and you're not, but they say the many are one. We all come into this world with an empty mind. Then it is indoctrinated with facts and beliefs. Verify! **Determination to evaluate the results of my beliefs, and its comparison with my intended results tells me that what I have been indoctrinated with has not given me full access to the abundance of this life.** How can the giver of life not be a respecter of person and then have a chosen people, conflict? How can the creator be both invisible with no name and the be an old European man with a beard and have a son from a dessert climate, and then doesn't have a tan? No man *hath seen God at any time.* —John 1:18. *For I have seen God face to face.* —Genesis 32:30, conflict. *For all have sinned and come short of the glory of God.* —Romans 3:23. *There was a man...who name was Job; and that man was perfect and upright.* —Job 1:1, conflict. A conflict simply means that the mind is confused between multiple perspectives/inclinations

38

and is not able to fixate on a singular vibration of thought. "If thine eye become single," abundance will follow. The resolution of conflicted vibrations in oneself results in the creation of a harmonious energy space which allows for a consistent mindset and thus creates a powerful force towards the creation of your desired reality. As a resurrected SOUL, the death of indoctrination, is the birth of imagination. Life is our teacher; we go where no man/woman has gone before. We project the high frequency of love, light, and gratitude regardless of the circumstances and abundance returns to us, this is the law of attraction. I AM forever grateful. I can and will attract all things through my imagination (spiritual mind) that strengthens and guides me, by saying "YES" to life, living my intention, planting some beauty every day, and counting all costs. I AM, one creator (the individual authority over my life and decisions), one Soul (the individualized consciousness of source energy), made from one blood, one flesh, one spirit. I AM at ONE I and my creator. (SOURCE) are one. All is one.

the Way of Consciousness

(…)

Why did this happen to me? The mechanical analysis of events only deals with the external relationship of things, (things which are seen, are not made of things that do appear). The meaning and cause of life comes from the consciousness of man/women. Reality comes from the invisible. In biblical allegories, when a stone blocks the well, it means that the people have taken the great symbolic revelations of truth literally. When someone rolls away the stone, it means that the individual has discovered beneath the allegory or parable its psychological life meaning. I AM forever grateful. I can and will attract all things through my imagination (spiritual mind) that strengthens and guides me, by saying "YES" to life, living my intention, planting some beauty every day, and counting all costs. I AM, one creator (the individual authority over my life and decisions), one Soul (the individualized consciousness of source energy), made from one blood, one

flesh, one spirit. I AM at ONE I and my creator. (SOURCE) are one. All is one.
the Way of Consciousness

(...)

How does energy transfer, transmute, and transform? Energy moves/transfers from one place to another. The spirit mind (Moses) called energy/god/SOURCE the all-consuming burning bush. It's either negative or positive but cannot be destroyed. Take a few deep breaths and thank the Universe, all beings that are working for the highest good of the planet and for helping to transmute negative energies for all beings that need love/positivism. Become a walking transmuter of negative SOURCE energy, grounded in the planet! If negative energy is not transmuted it will be transferred to those in closest proximity. Negative energy is transmuted/transformed with love. Transformation makes you different, you feel different about yourself, you begin to act accordingly and project to the world a different you. Transformation is a feeling that must be guarded. Transmutation changes the state of your nature. Rid yourself of the parts of self that no longer serve your highest good. Love is the key. However, you can only know the experience of love through your own personal experiences, not just those told by others. With love as the focal point the spirit man/woman is freed from the flesh and is able to rise above the earth-bound perspective and see a much larger existence. This is what is meant by turn the other cheek, you don't fight fire with fire! Don't be a part of the transfer, transmute or transform. I AM forever grateful. I can and will attract all things through my imagination (spiritual mind) that strengthens and guides me, by saying "YES" to life, living my intention, planting some beauty every day, and counting all costs. I AM, one creator (the individual authority over my life and decisions), one Soul (the individualized consciousness of source energy), made from one blood, one flesh, one spirit. I AM at ONE I and my creator. (SOURCE) are one. All is one.
the Way of Consciousness

(...)

The rejuvenating and reproducing power of the All in All in all of us comes from love, the All in All. Love is the "LIFE FORCE." When you deny love, you deny life. When, where, and why did you leave love? You can't leave love, it is the creation vibration, you can only suppress it. The allegorical devil /darkness in you suppresses it. The love vibration lifts us to a higher state of consciousness and frees us of the thoughts, feelings, and actions that minimize and victimize us. This means when you are vibrating at a low-level frequency/the devil/darkness in you will attract low-level painful experiences. When you are vibrating at a higher level frequency such as that of love and abundance, you will attract high-level experiences. To maintain the feeling of love is the key to health, happiness, and prosperity. When we maintain the actions that bring forth love as traditionally called the fruits of the spirit/the love vibration/god/SOURCE, our internal energy resonates at a high frequency and we express the god qualities of compassion, forgiveness, tolerance, respect, generosity, joy, peace, all that inspires, empowers, and enhances life. So, if you want success in your life work on raising your vibration, gone will be fear, guilt, judgment, greed, envy, arrogance, and the ego's stubborn need to be right. See yourself as LOVE (connected). I AM forever grateful. I can and will attract all things through my imagination (spiritual mind) that strengthens and guides me, by saying "YES" to life, living my intention, planting some beauty every day, and counting all costs. I AM, one creator (the individual authority over my life and decisions), one Soul (the individualized consciousness of source energy), made from one blood, one flesh, one spirit. I AM at ONE I and my creator. (SOURCE) are one. All is one.

the Way of Consciousness

(…)

All is mind. "There is no greater gift that anyone one can give than to lay down his or her life for a brother or sister. We are not talking about a physical life here, but a rebirth. The bible and other spiritual books attempt to relate what takes place in the mind/spiritual realm as the forerunner to realty. People take this stuff literally. It's all allegory! Reality begins in the mind. All reality first takes place in the world of SOURCE/the mind of god, the spiritual realm. The life you lay down for your brother or sister is the life of the indoctrinated mind, it is not you, it is the role you chose. It is a spiritual state of consciousness. A state of consciousness is a sense of one's personal or collective identity including beliefs about oneself. It is the state of the conscious mind. The boy lays down his child indoctrinated mind to become a young man, He no longer plays with toys. The young single man lays down his indoctrination to be a husband, he no longer plays with women. The couple lays down the honeymoon life to become parents, to build something for their children. An enlisted man/woman lays down their civilian life to become soldiers. The actor/actress lays down his/her life to play a role. It's all mind. Are you willing to lay down any of your indoctrination for the sake of humanity/a better world for everyone or just even a better world for yourself? Chose to be great, chose to be wealthy, choose to be loving, all these are states of mind that can be achieved with a change in perception/mindset. THINK BIG, then conscious reality evolves through practice and works as a gateway to the processing unit of the brain. It's all belief. It's all mind. I AM forever grateful. I can and will attract all things through my imagination (spiritual mind) that strengthens and guides me, by saying "YES" to life, living my intention, planting some beauty every day, and counting all costs. I AM, one creator (the individual authority over my life and decisions), one Soul (the individualized consciousness of source energy), made from one blood, one flesh, one spirit. I AM at ONE I and my creator. (SOURCE) are one. All is one.

the Way of Consciousness

(…)

Think in terms of energy. When judging others, we spend energy for no purpose. Do not eat of the tree of knowledge of good and evil (don't judge). Eat of the tree of life. Judgement polarizes itself. It keeps you from flowing through creation. It's

42

like you are throwing little rocks or sometimes even boulders into a stream, eventually blocking the whole stream, and thus creating stagnation in your life. This stagnation can show up in many ways, disease, depression, etc. The key to manifesting is letting go of the need to judge, it creates freedom of expression. Your judgement is negative energy, the repercussions of which you have termed a lack of light, darkness, the devil. Darkness, the devil is only a lack of light. Can you live your life without judging mine? When you judge others, you do not define them you define yourself. When we judge ourselves, our labor, or energy is always to our profit. Think in terms of energy. I AM forever grateful. I can and will attract all things through my imagination (spiritual mind) that strengthens and guides me, by saying "YES" to life, living my intention, planting some beauty every day, and counting all costs. I AM, one creator (the individual authority over my life and decisions), one Soul (the individualized consciousness of source energy), made from one blood, one flesh, one spirit. I AM at ONE I and my creator. (SOURCE) are one. All is one.

the Way of Consciousness

(…)

The law of attraction means when you are vibrating at a low-level frequency you will attract painful low-level experiences and when you are vibrating at a higher-level frequency such as that of love and abundance you will attract high-level experiences. So, who are you going to blame if it is your vibration/the devil/darkness in you that brings you your reality? The comedian Flip Wilson used to say, "The devil made me do it.". We are all in the same game just different levels, dealing with the same things, just different devils. Trust everyone, just don't trust the allegorical devil inside of everyone. The devil is a metaphor for negative energy. All is energy. The devil signifies the mass of thoughts that have built up in consciousness through many generations of earthy experience and crystalized into what may be termed human personality, or the carnal mind. What was the focal event that made you respond differently than love (positive energy)? When a person

43

does something wrong, they need to be punished, you believe in punitive justice, not restorative justice? This is your mindset, your belief. But when you are found in error you don't understand why you are punished, it is your belief being honored. When you believe in punitive justice you receive punishment. When you believe in restorative justice you are then restored. "It is done unto you as you believe." I AM forever grateful. I can and will attract all things through my imagination (spiritual mind) that strengthens and guides me, by saying "YES" to life, living my intention, planting some beauty every day, and counting all costs. I AM, one creator (the individual authority over my life and decisions), one Soul (the individualized consciousness of source energy), made from one blood, one flesh, one spirit. I AM at ONE I and my creator. (SOURCE) are one. All is one.

the Way of Consciousness

(...)

The duality of reality. Everything exists in polar opposites. All exist in two extremes, and you will receive the extreme you focus on. Living in a dualistic level of reality means there will always be both **positive and negative**, both good and bad. This being the case, wisdom dictates a re-evaluation of your core biological strategy that moves you toward the positive and away from the negative as a way to find happiness and peace. Regardless of how you understand it from the Divine perspective, how do you navigate the presence of positive and negative without setting up what you like against what you dislike (which is equivalent to suffering) since both will always be with you? "If thine eye become single." Walk in your FOCUS and FOCUS on your purpose, desires. The more you embrace and allow without judgement, the better it gets, good or bad. Focus on good, you get good. Focus on bad, you get bad. Focus on the problem, you get more problems. Focus on the solution, you get more solutions. Focus on what you want, not what you don't want. I AM forever grateful. I can and will attract all things through my imagination (spiritual mind) that strengthens and guides me, by saying "YES" to life, living my

44

intention, planting some beauty every day, and counting all costs. I AM, one creator (the individual authority over my life and decisions), one Soul (the individualized consciousness of source energy), made from one blood, one flesh, one spirit. I AM at ONE I and my creator. (SOURCE) are one. All is one. the Way of Consciousness

(…)

Stop chasing what the mind wants and you will get what your soul needs. Allow the story of your life to write itself. We are souls, the spiritual or immaterial part of a human being, regarded as immortal. The human soul is the part of a person that is not physical. It is the part of every human being that lasts eternally after the body experiences death. "You don't have a soul. You are a Soul. You have a body." In other words, personhood is not based on having a body. A soul is what is required. It is timeless, unconditionally loving presence within us. We find our purpose by reconnecting with our soul. When we live from the Soul, we are guided to understand our sacred life purpose. Live out of your soul, not your eyes. I AM forever grateful. I can and will attract all things through my imagination (spiritual mind) that strengthens and guides me, by saying "YES" to life, living my intention, planting some beauty every day, and counting all costs. I AM, one creator (the individual authority over my life and decisions), one Soul (the individualized consciousness of source energy), made from one blood, one flesh, one spirit. I AM at ONE I and my creator. (SOURCE) are one. All is one. the Way of Consciousness

(…)

Most of us have lost touch with the truth of who we are. We assume that we are our bodies, thoughts, feelings, beliefs, memories, and preferences because that is what we've been conditioned to believe since childhood. The journey of the soul is the path of reuniting you with your true nature, the body is the means of transportation, and the mind is a thought processor. The healthy life is one of

45

continuing spiritual, emotional, and relational growth. But so many of us feel stuck or stagnated at one stage of the journey. It's not always clear to us where or why we are stuck, making it difficult to take the next step on our journey of the soul resurrection. Spiritual books take us on a spiritual journey. Religion/stories/allegories/ parables turns the soul into characters so the concepts can be simplified. The Book of Revelation deals with the 7 seals/blockages to overcome/ that have to be opened to fulfill the soul journey on the physical plane; fear/guilt/shame/grief/lies/the illusion of separation and attachments. Life will continue to carry us through all of these blockages/ experiences until the soul is free. Break through, learn how to listen to and reclaim your True Nature, or Soul, then you experience what awakened beings through the ages have experienced, your Christ like nature, the ability to transcend suffering, embody unconditional love, peace and live authentically again. I AM forever grateful. I can and will attract all things through my imagination (spiritual mind) that strengthens and guides me, by saying "YES" to life, living my intention, planting some beauty every day, and counting all costs. I AM, one creator (the individual authority over my life and decisions), one Soul 1 (the individualized consciousness of source energy), made from one blood, one flesh, one spirit. I AM at ONE I and my creator. (SOURCE) are one. All is one. the Way of Consciousness

(…)

Indoctrination occurs when a person's capacity to rationally justify one's beliefs consider alternatives and make autonomous choices in life is paralyzed. Is a baby a human being? And of course, the answer is yes. But the baby has no focused thoughts, no indoctrination. The current consensus is that infants are thinking all the time, but busy trying to make sense of the world around them from the moment they emerge from the womb. This tells us that to be human has nothing to do with what we believe. You are not your beliefs. It's ok to give up your indoctrination if it is not working for you. It's ok to create a new

46

reality that benefits you. You don't have to defend your beliefs, they come and go. Being human means accepting all that you are and living your life in a way that brings forth joy and happiness, making the most of one's existence; to develop the ability to act or function independently. Develop your own mind and live abundantly within the reflection of your own goals, and perceptions. The happy baby never stops developing. I AM forever grateful. I can and will attract all things through my imagination (spiritual mind) that strengthens and guides me, by saying "YES" to life, living my intention, planting some beauty every day, and counting all costs. I AM, one creator (the individual authority over my life and decisions), one Soul (the individualized consciousness of source energy), made from one blood, one flesh, one spirit. I AM at ONE I and my creator. (SOURCE) are one. All is one. the Way of Consciousness

(…)

There are things that we learn and can know with our upbringing, facts, figures, words, phrases, how things relate to one another. These are all things we are taught. It's relatively easy to gain head knowledge. You can just study and spend time learning and then eventually over time your brain will collect more data. We know and operationalize this stuff out of memory. Then there are things that we know with our hearts, is *spiritually discerned*. Indoctrination is aimed at influencing people to believe in facts, without being able to back up these newfound facts with anything but opinion. You can be indoctrinated into a political party, a cult, or a religious belief system. In fact, all of us are indoctrinated into a belief system as we are growing up. Revelation knowledge is built on light and love. Once you realize that there are these two kinds of knowledge it takes the pressure off for living a life of the highest vibration/love. Instead of asking for more will power to destroy the things we disagree with and avoid evolving, ask for more revelation, it's the way to love. I AM forever grateful. I can and will attract all things through my imagination (spiritual mind) that strengthens and guides me, by saying "YES" to life, living my intention, planting some beauty every day, and counting all costs. I AM, one creator (the individual authority over my life and decisions), one Soul (the individualized consciousness of source energy), made from one blood, one flesh, one spirit. I AM at ONE I and my creator. (SOURCE) are one. All is one.

the Way of Consciousness

(...)

It is a story about life. It is an allegory. Get in where you fit in. The eldest son Esau (Prince William) was entitled to the birthright by doctrine. It is easier for a pig to fly than for an established person to leave their indoctrination. Prince Harry (Jacob) questioned the doctrine and chose to forge his own path. Isaac (representing god) in this allegory says come close my son that I might feel you. Prince Harry (Jacob) moved close to Isaac (blind god) and is felt. The blessing goes to the one that can feel it because in real life god is blind and invisible. As a vibrational being God has to feel you. What is your limitation/ indoctrination, wrong cultural upbringing, not enough money, too young, too old, female, gay, not the oldest, criminal record, not the right time? You get what you can feel regardless of your circumstances. Believe it until you see it! Feel your desire. Your only limitation is your indoctrination. I AM forever grateful. I can and will attract all things through my imagination (spiritual mind) that strengthens and guides me, by saying "YES" to life, living my intention, planting some beauty every day, and counting all costs. I AM, one creator (the individual authority over my life and decisions), one Soul (the individualized consciousness of source energy), made from one blood, one flesh, one spirit. I AM at ONE I and my creator. (SOURCE) are one. All is one.

the Way of Consciousness

(...)

King James Version 7 "And the Lord God formed man of the dust of the ground, and breathed into his nostrils the breath of life; and man **became a living soul**." The soul is defined as

individualized god consciousness. God cannot leave or forsake itself. The soul (individualized god consciousness) is encapsulated in human flesh for the earthly sojourn. The flesh has legs and no sight, and the soul has sight and no legs. The indoctrinated mind will be led by the blind flesh to the challenges it needs, to become enlightened. The indoctrinated (in-dark-nation) flesh walks in darkness. To be saved is to awaken the soul while encapsulated in the flesh. This is the light. Walking in darkness will lead to physical death and returning home without ever comprehending one's soul/ divine nature/individualized god consciousness on the physical plane (you never regain the sight of the light). The individualized god consciousness/your divine nature/soul can be resurrected at any point in the sojourn. The mind and body are then understood for the tools they were originally designed for; to create whatever you can imagine by way of source (i-magi-nation), not man. The resurrected soul is the awakened god in you. It's called Christ, the awakened god within, enlightenment. It walks the earth, carried by the flesh defined not by indoctrination but light and love. I AM forever grateful. I can and will attract all things through my imagination (spiritual mind) that strengthens and guides me, by saying "YES" to life, living my intention, planting some beauty every day, and counting all costs. I AM, one creator (the individual authority over my life and decisions), one Soul (the individualized consciousness of source energy), made from one blood, one flesh, one spirit. I AM at ONE I and my creator. (SOURCE) are one. All is one.
the Way of Consciousness

(…)

Love and light is the answer. Light and love is the response to take you out of hell. KARMA is the force generated by a person's actions to perpetuate the cause of going from one mental state to another and in its ethical consequences to determine the nature of the person's next experience. Blame it on the devil! KARMA in actuality is the force considered as affecting the events of one's life. Sexual/mutual attraction plays a role in the next experience. We don't get what we want

we get what we deserve, exactly the consequences of what we have put out. It is the light journey of the soul. We will attract whatever it takes for the soul to balance our love and light. Whatever you respond with will come back home. The more you resolve conflict with light and love, the more light and love you will receive. Get to know the soul, it is your life's teacher. And whenever the teacher gives a pop quiz, (brings you an experience), the answer is love and light. It is called enlightenment/higher learning. I AM forever grateful. I can and will attract all things through my imagination (spiritual mind) that strengthens and guides me, by saying "YES" to life, living my intention, planting some beauty every day, and counting all costs. I AM, one creator (the individual authority over my life and decisions), one Soul (the individualized consciousness of source energy), made from one blood, one flesh, one spirit. I AM at ONE I and my creator. (SOURCE) are one. All is one.
the Way of Consciousness

(…)

Compassion is a reflex of the open heart, not a thought, but a feeling. The thought comes with how one responds to the reflex action/feeling of compassion. Compassion comes from the heart, benevolence comes from the thought. The benevolent response carries compassion from being about the other person to being about you. Benevolence is about your charity or doing good deeds and what you think about it. Compassion is concern for sufferings and/or the misfortunes of others. A word of encouragement or even a hug is always an applicable act of compassion. It is the action of giving someone support that counts, and not how much. It's always appropriate to give directions/ confidence to one lost. I AM forever grateful. I can and will attract all things through my imagination (spiritual mind) that strengthens and guides me, by saying "YES" to life, living my intention, planting some beauty every day, and counting all costs. I AM, one creator (the individual authority over my life and decisions), one Soul (the individualized consciousness of source energy), made from one blood, one
50

flesh, one spirit. I AM at ONE I and my creator. (SOURCE) are one. All is one.
the Way of Consciousness

(…)

Cinco de Mayo is an annual celebration held on May 5th. The date is observed to commemorate the Mexican Army's victory over the French Empire, on May 5, 1862. The fourth of July, Independence Day, is a holiday in the US commemorating the Declaration of Independence of the United States, on July 4, 1776. The September 11th attacks, referred to as 9/11, were a series of attacks against the United States on Tuesday, September 11, 2001. These are historical events that are actually celebrated on the historical dates in which they happened. Easter for the year 2019 was celebrated on Sunday, April 21st, April 12, 2020, April 04, 2021… and March 31,2024. Each year Easter has been determined to fall on the Sunday after the full moon. But how? It has no historical date because it is not a historical event. All the details of the supposed historical crucifixion of Jesus are symbols, carefully designed to paint a vivid *allegorical* picture of the tests and trials of human initiation and symbolizes what we all must go through to evolve. It is the Higher Self of the Initiate—the Christ-principle in us *all,* crucified on the cross of wooden ignorance and intolerance. Death of the old man/woman, birth of the spirit walk. This year, gain a deeper insight. I AM forever grateful. I can and will attract all things through my imagination (spiritual mind) that strengthens and guides me, by saying "YES" to life, living my intention, planting some beauty every day, and counting all costs. I AM, one creator (the individual authority over my life and decisions), one Soul (the individualized consciousness of source energy), made from one blood, one flesh, one spirit. I AM at ONE I and my creator. (SOURCE) are one. All is one.
the Way of Consciousness

(…)

Easter follows the March equinox, it is a celebration of life characterized in the allegory/myth of Jesus. It is the experience of rebirth. First, it is not the past that determines our current experience; it is our thought about the past determining our current experience. That's because a thought cannot be in the past. If we have any thoughts moving through our mind, and we constantly do, they are right now affecting every aspect of our being, physically, mentally, and emotionally. Right now, we're either getting better or worse, depending on what we're giving our attention to. It's not the past doing this, it's our present thinking about the past that affects our life. We have the ability to name things, we can name it all good. When we do that, our life begins to immediately change because *as within, so without*. Easter is an opportunity to be reborn into a new life, renew thoughts and feelings. The beginning of Spring/ the March equinox is the most important moment of the year because it celebrates the resurrection of all nature It is in the present moment that the Christ presence returns. When we realize that the Christ is not a person, but that part of God in all of us, we become fully aware that Jesus, the man, is not coming back, the Christ presence within us is and returns when we allow it to be the activity of our awareness. When we do, we live with awareness, understanding that which is within us. Raise the dead you! I AM forever grateful. I can and will attract all things through my imagination (spiritual mind) that strengthens and guides me, by saying "YES" to life, living my intention, planting some beauty every day, and counting all costs. I AM, one creator (the individual authority over my life and decisions), one Soul (the individualized consciousness of source energy), made from one blood, one flesh, one spirit. I AM at ONE I and my creator. (SOURCE) are one. All is one. the Way of Consciousness

(…)

How can you live with certainty in an uncertain world? Revelation leads to the light, a higher level of consciousness. In-dark-nation/indoctrination/ego keeps you where you are. Detach, in detachment lies the wisdom of uncertainty. In the
52

wisdom of uncertainty lies the freedom from our past, from the known, which is the prison of past conditioning. And in our willingness to step into the unknown field of all possibilities we surrender ourselves to the creative mind, that orchestrates the dance of the universe. Detachment is experiencing our feelings without letting them control us. We step away from harmful cravings. We detach from others knowing that their spiritual work is not ours to do. We choose how we will act rather than reacting. Detachment allows us to be in the world but not of the world, it frees us to live our lives with grace! I AM forever grateful. I can and will attract all things through my imagination (spiritual mind) that strengthens and guides me, by saying "YES" to life, living my intention, planting some beauty every day, and counting all costs. I AM, one creator (the individual authority over my life and decisions), one Soul (the individualized consciousness of source energy), made from one blood, one flesh, one spirit. I AM at ONE I and my creator. (SOURCE) are one. All is one.

the Way of Consciousness

(…)

Throughout human existence each myth, religious book is/has been a metaphor for life. A figure of speech in which words, people, places, and phrases are applied to an object or action to which it is not literally applicable (dead men don't get up, souls do). A thing regarded as representative or symbolic of something else, especially something abstract or invisible. Metaphor is important because it helps to explain your life/the human journey in other, simpler, terms. You are the savior/hero of your story. Save yourself! Myths are universal, all novels, all movies, all religious text suggest the hero's/savior's journey or stay a victim, living without complete understanding/an unfulfilled life/wasteland. **The call**, the reluctant hero, **separation**, fear. **Threshold crossing,** magical helper, road of trials, night sea journey, adventure, initiation. **Threshold crossing,** apotheosis (the elevation to divine status, celebrity; deification), enter the cave, courage, helpers, belly of the whale. **Threshold crossing,** rescue, test, dragon battle, magical flight. **Return, treasure (**the story is told to the people and they reject it). It is the same thread in all cultures. All souls (the individual consciousness of god) must travel their own journey! No priest, preacher, teacher or savior can walk my journey for me, they only point the WAY. I AM forever grateful. I can and will attract all things through my imagination (spiritual mind) that strengthens and guides me, by saying "YES" to life, living my intention, planting some beauty every day, and counting all costs. I AM, one creator (the individual authority over my life and decisions), one Soul (the individualized consciousness of source energy), made from one blood, one flesh, one spirit. I AM at ONE I and my creator. (SOURCE) are one. All is one. the Way of Consciousness

(…)

We each have a divine nature and destiny. Evolve or repeat. My success is based on my ability to evolve. My success is predicated upon my alignment with Source energy. All is energy and the LIFE FORCE of SOURCE is LOVE. SOURCE provides everything on the planet and uses every resource necessary to fulfill my desires with the necessary people, places, and things for expansion. We all are a bundle of energy being directed by thoughts and will be used in the greatest capacity to expand the planet. Don't get caught up in personalities, think in terms of the energy a particular personality brings to evolve you. No thing nor person can come into your life except through you/your thoughts, all for the purpose of your evolution/expansion. You are the door, "I AM, only because you are." "It is drawn unto thee through the divine nature. Remember who you were before the world told you who you should be. I AM forever grateful. I can and will attract all things through my imagination (spiritual mind) that strengthens and guides me, by saying "YES" to life, living my intention, planting some beauty every day, and counting all costs. I AM, one creator (the individual authority over my life and decisions), one Soul (the individualized consciousness of source energy), made from one blood, one flesh, one spirit. I AM at ONE I and my creator. (SOURCE) are one. All is one. the Way of Consciousness

54

(…)

The whole point of being alive is to evolve. The energy you need to transform into a new reality will manifest in physical form, unfolding and complimenting your existing physical reality/your mindset. If an existing physical manifestation does not evolve with you to higher levels of consciousness as it must, choosing to repeat instead, another physical manifestation awaits your new evolutionary state on the next plane. It's all one energy on different frequencies of lower and higher consciousness. Don't settle for less than your vision. Evolve into the complete person you were meant to be. I will give an overabundance of love and play fair. It's all energy and I get what I give! Evolve or repeat, but I'm not repeating with you. And I will always love you. I AM forever grateful. I can and will attract all things through my imagination (spiritual mind) that strengthens and guides me, by saying "YES" to life, living my intention, planting some beauty every day, and counting all costs. I AM, one creator (the individual authority over my life and decisions), one Soul (the individualized consciousness of source energy), made from one blood, one flesh, one spirit. I AM at ONE I and my creator. (SOURCE) are one. All is one.

the Way of Consciousness

(…)

Are you on a path of indoctrination or a path of divination? Start with a cage containing five apes. In the cage, hang a banana on a string and put stairs under it. Before long, an ape will start to climb towards the banana. As soon as he touches the stairs, spray all of the apes with cold water. After a while, another ape makes an attempt with the same result. If, later, another ape tries to climb the stairs, the other apes will try to prevent it even though no water sprays them. Now, remove one ape from the cage and replace him with a new one. The new ape sees the banana and starts to climb the stairs. To his horror, all of the other apes attack him. After another attempt and attack, he knows that if he tries to climb the stairs, he will be assaulted.

55

Next, remove another of the original five apes and replace it with a new one. The newcomer goes to the stairs and is attacked. The previous newcomer takes part in the punishment with enthusiasm. Again, replace a third original ape with a new one. The new one makes it to the stairs and is attacked as well. Two of the four apes that beat him have no idea why they were not permitted to climb the stairs, or why they are participating in the beating of the newest ape. After replacing the fourth and fifth original apes, all the apes which have been sprayed with cold water have been replaced. Nevertheless, no ape/monkey mind ever again approaches the stairs. Why not? "Because that's the way it's always been around here. That is how organization behavior is indoctrinated into policy and culture becomes entrenched. I AM forever grateful. I can and will attract all things through my imagination (spiritual mind) that strengthens and guides me, by saying "YES" to life, living my intention, planting some beauty every day, and counting all costs. I AM, one creator (the individual authority over my life and decisions), one Soul (the individualized consciousness of source energy), made from one blood, one flesh, one spirit. I AM at ONE I and my creator. (SOURCE) are one. All is one. the Way of Consciousness

(…)

Alicia Keyes said her overnight success was 10 years in the making. Nothing happens overnight but then again, it is over the next night. You wake up one day and it's there. The super power is focus. All is mind. Make up your mind and don't be swayed. It is the process of divination. Divination is the process of drawing in the divine power through attention on that which you desire. Your thoughts are now focused. If wearing number 32 like Jim Brown focuses your attention on being a great football player then that is divination, it draws out your god given abilities with thoughts of greatness. If wearing diamonds and furs and driving a nice car keeps your focus on having nice things, that's divination. Writing everyday keeps me focused on publishing, it has to happen. The focus brings it to pass. And then someone with no focus tells me to go get a job. I choose to

56

stay focused and let my overnight success be ten years in the making, or one year. The invisible, behind the scenes divine actions become visible. Everything came from the invisible. I AM forever grateful. I can and will attract all things through my imagination (spiritual mind) that strengthens and guides me, by saying "YES" to life, living my intention, planting some beauty every day, and counting all costs. I AM, one creator (the individual authority over my life and decisions), one Soul (the individualized consciousness of source energy), made from one blood, one flesh, one spirit. I AM at ONE I and my creator. (SOURCE) are one. All is one. the Way of Consciousness

(...)

How can I say anything about your mother or a loved one if I don't know your mother or loved one? You know your mother intimately, and therefore will stand and testify on what she stands for, her living testimony. When explained, all near death experiences feature light. Light is everywhere the symbol of joy and of life-giving power. In all civilizations light passes from being a physical phenomenon to being a symbolic archetype. In ancient Egyptian culture the radiance of light accompanies the first cosmic dawn. In other words, God is light. God's living testimony is love and light. Any book/ person that interprets god as other than love and light to all humanity misinterprets god. The Holy Qur'an describes God as the "Light of the heavens and earth." In Buddhism, God Almighty (Brahman) resides within all humans as Light, a fact supported by all scripture. Biblical references: 1 John 1:5, Psalm 44:3, Ezekiel 1:28, Ezekiel 1:27, Ezekiel 8:2, Psalm 94:1, and Psalm 50:2. In Hinduism, light symbolizes Brahman, the eye, the individual Self, gods, divinity, purity, supreme bliss, divine power, divine quality, any heavenly body. Get to know god for yourself before your culture indoctrinates about who god is. Yes, god is revealed through culture and every culture defines god as light. Know that god is light and love before you start accepting allegorical misinterpretations about god from the pulpit/anywhere. I AM forever grateful. I can and will attract all things through my

imagination (spiritual mind) that strengthens and guides me, by saying "YES" to life, living my intention, planting some beauty every day, and counting all costs. I AM, one creator (the individual authority over my life and decisions), one Soul (the individualized consciousness of source energy), made from one blood, one flesh, one spirit. I AM at ONE I and my creator. (SOURCE) are one. All is one.
the Way of Consciousness

(…)

Returning to the divine state, becoming a god man/god woman is to but re-member. With our selfishness and our ego, we create the disharmony within ourselves and in the world. Whatever energy we put out into the world is reflected back in the form of karma. Don't look for a devil, look at what you put out. The suffering/pain we receive is a free-will choice, it is a reflection of what we put out in the universe so as to see ourselves and our actions. Unfortunately, many of us believe our trials come from out of nowhere. Many are blind and cannot see, and many don't want to see. Trials have a history. The journey to becoming a god man/woman begins with understanding where our personal trials come from. We suffer to draw attention to our weaknesses, identifying what we need to work on. Faith is not enough. Belief in a savior does not end suffering. Suffering is a result of emotional responses indoctrinated and formed into habits. Cause and effect. Whatever you inflict upon another you inflict upon yourself, it's the way you learn all is one. When the trials of habit cause enough pain the effect of wanting to change direction occurs. I'm woke now! I AM ready to follow the guiding spirit. I AM forever grateful. I can and will attract all things through my imagination (spiritual mind) that strengthens and guides me, by saying "YES" to life, living my intention, planting some beauty every day, and counting all costs. I AM, one creator (the individual authority over my life and decisions), one Soul (the individualized consciousness of source energy), made from one blood, one flesh, one spirit. I AM at ONE I and my creator. (SOURCE) are one. All is one.
the Way of Consciousness

All of our knowledge is the offspring of our perceptions. "You are the root and the offspring." The root/the Father is your subconscious mind and is the underground/unseen part of the seed of conception, created reality. The plant body/offspring is supported by the root that originates everything in your life. It functions as an organ of absorption, aeration, and storage or as a means of anchorage and support for what you experience. Know what you are planting, it will launch. The offspring comes into existence as a result of your thinking patterns. It is what you laid down in your mind. Everything outside of nature is the offspring of an idea. I and my Father are one, the root and the offspring are one, it's all one. I can do nothing except the Father/subconscious mind ordains it. The mind is a tool, use your mind, stop letting your mind use you. Believing is seeing. I AM forever grateful. I can and will attract all things through my imagination (spiritual mind) that strengthens and guides me, by saying "YES" to life, living my intention, planting some beauty every day, and counting all costs. I AM, one creator (the individual authority over my life and decisions), one Soul (the individualized consciousness of source energy), made from one blood, one flesh, one spirit. I AM at ONE I and my creator. (SOURCE) are one. All is one. the Way of Consciousness

(…)

_____ is the reason I can't succeed. A scape goat is a person who is blamed for the wrongdoings, mistakes, or faults of others. The term 'scapegoat' actually has its origin in the Old Testament, more specifically, in **Chapter 16 of the Book of Leviticus**, according to which God instructed Moses and Aaron to sacrifice two goats every year. The first goat was to be killed and its blood sprinkled upon the Ark of the Covenant for the symbolic removal of the people's sins with the literal removal of the second goat, outcast in the desert as part of the ceremonies of the Day of Atonement. Today, Jesus is supposedly the scape goat that eliminates your bad Karma and makes life heaven on earth. News flash, your bad Karma will come back to you and your good karma will come back to you. It is the Universal law of Cause and Effect. That's the way of the world, Jesus or Jedi. The very essence of a scape goat signals there are some who are chronically avoiding responsibility for their actions. God is the most popular scape goat of all time for our sins with the devil running a close second. Be willing to face the truth within yourself and right your own wrongs. I AM forever grateful. I can and will attract all things through my imagination (spiritual mind) that strengthens and guides me, by saying "YES" to life, living my intention, planting some beauty every day, and counting all costs. I AM, one creator (the individual authority over my life and decisions), one Soul (the individualized consciousness of source energy), made from one blood, one flesh, one spirit. I AM at ONE I and my creator. (SOURCE) are one. All is one. the Way of Consciousness

(…)

There is a saying "you become what you judge". Have you seen this happen to anyone? Have you ever noticed somebody judging and then they have become what they judged? When you help someone while judging them, you are loving them conditionally. The condition being that they would be better with your view of how they should be. You are fulfilling your own beliefs and needs. You cannot know what another soul needs to learn and grow. Some believe that when you judge others you take on their karma. In other words, the more you judge the more you need to resolve the issues you are judging. You can just love them as they are and help them when they indicate by some form that they want the assistance. Judging others is about you, not them, it makes you feel better about the things you have been indoctrinated to believe. Love neighbor the same way you love self and don't judge. I think that about wraps up a well lived life. I AM forever grateful. I can and will attract all things through my imagination (spiritual mind) that strengthens and guides me, by saying "YES" to life, living my intention, planting some beauty every day, and counting all
60

costs. I AM, one creator (the individual authority over my life and decisions), one Soul (the individualized consciousness of source energy), made from one blood, one flesh, one spirit. I AM at ONE I and my creator. (SOURCE) are one. All is one. the Way of Consciousness

(…)

You are an eternal being, your only limitation is your indoctrination. Okay, we see the paths and we see the road less traveled. The road less traveled is the unknown/imagination. When you travel into the unknown god takes you there. Here are the choices; hard work, privilege, poverty, prosperity, or the road less traveled /love/ light/and posterity. Respond with the indoctrinated/monkey mind/what you know, ups and downs/ doors close, darkness, you get a cage. Light and love is not bound by time or limitations, it is eternal. The road less traveled, light/love leads to posterity has no opposite, thine eye becomes single. Just follow your dream, respond to every time bound experience with light and love and doors open, you fly. It's like going on a ride, exciting, always revealing something new, and always taking you to a higher level of consciousness. When we are planning for posterity, we ought to remember that virtue is not hereditary. I AM forever grateful. I can and will attract all things through my imagination (spiritual mind) that strengthens and guides me, by saying "YES" to life, living my intention, planting some beauty every day, and counting all costs. I AM, one creator (the individual authority over my life and decisions), one Soul (the individualized consciousness of source energy), made from one blood, one flesh, one spirit. I AM at ONE I and my creator. (SOURCE) are one. All is one. the Way of Consciousness

(…)

Mules are always boasting that their ancestors were horses. Hip hop was created for us by us through the human imagination portal. Before hip hop, the music/talent of the ancestors was/is harvested in our communities like cotton was on the plantation. "You pick the cotton; we'll make the T-shirts." Stop being a mule to carry someone else's vision/cotton. You discover your ministry/purpose through your life experiences. If you can learn from the worst times in your life/mistakes, you'll be ready to go into the best times of your life. Mistakes are the portals of discovery. The goat has fear in front, it's in back of a mule, and on every side of a fool. Fear not, until you are broken, you don't know what you're made of. It gives you the opportunity to meet your ability face to face, then give your testimony/your story, it's your ministry. One stupid mistake can change everything. I AM forever grateful. I can and will attract all things through my imagination (spiritual mind) that strengthens and guides me, by saying "YES" to life, living my intention, planting some beauty every day, and counting all costs. I AM, one creator (the individual authority over my life and decisions), one Soul (the individualized consciousness of source energy), made from one blood, one flesh, one spirit. I AM at ONE I and my creator. (SOURCE) are one. All is one. the Way of Consciousness

(…)

In the fictional movie "Gremlins" the original story shows both the light and dark side of these cuddly animals. The light of god is in all of us, it resides as our soul. The soul is covered by flesh and until it is resurrected darkness will prevail. The resurrection is not a one time, one savior job! When all a person knows is darkness how do you expect them to respond to life? Thug life is a term used with pride, to describe a person who started out with nothing and built themselves up to be something. Tupac explains that the Acronym Thug Life : **The Hate U Give Little Infants Fucks Everybody.** It means that society harms itself and everyone if it does not love its youngest members. So, then we accept the government-sanctioned affirmative action program called Jim Crow, which includes rape/ lynching's/dehumanization/darkness, and then government says affirmative action/light is bad to rectify the harm caused.

Until the soul is resurrected in individuals, no matter the race, color, gender or nationality, people will be prone to respond with light and love in situations where peace and patience reside and will be prone to violent outburst where hate and harm reside. We are all victims and victors of our circumstances. If I fall prey to a moment of anger, don't kill me before I face the true justice, the rule of law. I AM forever grateful. I can and will attract all things through my imagination (spiritual mind) that strengthens and guides me, by saying "YES" to life, living my intention, planting some beauty every day, and counting all costs. I AM, one creator (the individual authority over my life and decisions), one Soul (the individualized consciousness of source energy), made from one blood, one flesh, one spirit. I AM at ONE I and my creator. (SOURCE) are one. All is one. the Way of Consciousness

(…)

Darkness cannot live in the light; it will always try to put out the light. If a person cannot see the light of god in themselves, how do you expect them to see the light of god in you? An indoctrinated /monkey mind can only see god where they have been told/trained to see god. The native Americans were annihilated because their killer/exterminators were told there was no god in them (heathens). YET God is invisible, god is spirit, and god has blond hair and blue eyes (indoctrination/in-dark-nation). The only way to survive the dark hearted is to treat those indoctrinated in darkness, the uncivilized in a civilized way. Malcolm told King, "I don't agree, we are human beings." King responded, "Malcolm, the native Americans were human beings also." The 1921 massacre of blacks in Tulsa, Oklahoma bears witness that we must first gain our civil rights (equal protection under the law) in the mist of this darkness, before we declare our human rights, or we will be slaughtered like the native Americans. Still, our brothers and sisters will be singled out for death, but Civil rights is a government shield against our mass murder/genocide. It's our only hope, hold on to the vision, trust the process. I AM forever grateful. I can and will attract all things through my imagination (spiritual mind) that strengthens and guides me, by saying "YES" to life, living my intention, planting some beauty every day, and counting all costs. I AM, one creator (the individual authority over my life and decisions), one Soul (the individualized consciousness of source energy), made from one blood, one flesh, one spirit. I AM at ONE I and my creator. (SOURCE) are one. All is one. the Way of Consciousness

(…)

The universal life force is love, period.
The life force is love. God is love. All other theological conversation/discussion/interpretation is about nothing. The Jewish nation are not the chosen people. God is not a respecter of person. Anyone can get a blessing, not just the Jewish nation. The chosen people/thoughts are called Israelites. The Israelite is a mind that recognizes god and follows the soul. A gentile is a mind that does not know god. Neither the gentiles nor the Israelites are a race of physical people but terms used to identify the mind that affirms the spiritual substance and life force as love and those that don't. Love is the root that sustains all life. When one responds to any situation with any response other than love (the life force) they are left unprotected /vulnerable to mishaps, stray bullets, accidents. They are left disconnected from love (the root) for as long as they refuse to embrace it. When a tree is disconnected from its root the leaves fall off, the same with you and I. When we are disconnected from the root/love our wheels fall off. Just as the tree is sustained by the root that are not visible, the soul is sustained by the creator, the root of all existence, the invisible god. The tree and the root cannot be separated, neither can the soul be separated from the root (love), I and my father/creator/sustainer are one. Beware of the theologian, they talk in the temples, however Love is an expression of the mind. I AM forever grateful. I can and will attract all things through my imagination (spiritual mind) that strengthens and guides me, by saying "YES" to life, living my
64

intention, planting some beauty every day, and counting all costs. I AM, one creator (the individual authority over my life and decisions), one Soul (the individualized consciousness of source energy), made from one blood, one flesh, one spirit. I AM at ONE I and my creator. (SOURCE) are one. All is one. the Way of Consciousness

(…)

Whatever lies ahead of me, god is already there. What is god? If by that question we mean, what is god like in herself/himself/itself/god-self, there is no answer. If by the question we mean, what has god disclosed about god-self that relevant reason can comprehend, there is, I believe an answer both full and satisfying. God is! God is the power that animates (brings to life) every atom, every molecule, every cell, every stone, every star, every planet, every plant, every animal, and yes you, god animates you also. God is like the ocean, you can see traces of its beginning but not its end. Only a fool will tell you where god ends or who god ends with. God is omnipotent and omnipresent, always has been, always will be. That means god in everywhere at all times. You can never go where god is not. The best thing of all is that god is in all of us. Those who see god in everything will eventually see everything in god. The All in All. When you comprehend this revelation, then you can say without hesitation, the consciousness of humankind has risen through me. I have risen from the dead. I and my father are one. I AM forever grateful. I can and will attract all things through my imagination (spiritual mind) that strengthens and guides me, by saying "YES" to life, living my intention, planting some beauty every day, and counting all costs. I AM, one creator (the individual authority over my life and decisions), one Soul (the individualized consciousness of source energy), made from one blood, one flesh, one spirit. I AM at ONE I and my creator. (SOURCE) are one. All is one. the Way of Consciousness

(…)

Matthew Henson was one of the era's few African American explorers, and he may have been the first man, black or white, to reach the North Pole. He didn't only read about the North Pole, he experienced it. We are here to experience the physical realm, reality. The information and materials are here for us to experience whatever it is we can imagine, focus (our super power), count the costs, strike out. My imagination is my savior. I desire to experience god for myself. My soul is not bound by time, it takes flight into eternity and travels throughout the night seeking solutions to my time bound experiences. I AM an explorer, a social scientist. My soul goes into the spiritual realm through meditation and sleep and brings back information from source that is accessible to anyone willing to travel the spiritual path. Henry Ford went there and discovered the materials and resources to design and build an automobile. Steve Jobs, the iPhone. I capture information and bring it back so as to make it assessable to all with open hearts and listening ears, yearning to awaken. I AM forever grateful. I can and will attract all things through my imagination (spiritual mind) that strengthens and guides me, by saying "YES" to life, living my intention, planting some beauty every day, and counting all costs. I AM, one creator (the individual authority over my life and decisions), one Soul (the individualized consciousness of source energy), made from one blood, one flesh, one spirit. I AM at ONE I and my creator. (SOURCE) are one. All is one.

the Way of Consciousness

(…)

The soul is eternal, existing both before and after death. The soul is the individualized consciousness of god experiencing godself, much like we experience ourselves through the cells and organisms that make up our body. Plato likened the soul to a charioteer in charge of two horses, the mind and the body, which are pulling in completely opposite directions. The soul wanting to go back to the world of creating forms/beauty and the body wanting to enjoy the five senses plus pleasure. So, what is the significance of such a temporary life? The body is deigned

66

to derive pleasure in many subtle ways. Only a human stops to enjoy a sunset or to appreciate a bird's song. With the makeup of the body, we appreciate beauty through sight, sound, smell, touch, and taste. So what is the destination it has to reach when the soul leaves the body? I believe it gains control of the mind and body, living the beauty of each precious moment, where god truly experiences godself. The actual self is the soul, while the body is only a mechanism to experience the karma of that life. I AM forever grateful. I can and will attract all things through my imagination (spiritual mind) that strengthens and guides me, by saying "YES" to life, living my intention, planting some beauty every day, and counting all costs. I AM, one creator (the individual authority over my life and decisions), one Soul (the individualized consciousness of source energy), made from one blood, one flesh, one spirit. I AM at ONE I and my creator. (SOURCE) are one. All is one. the Way of Consciousness

(…)

Religion is an experience of the mind and body. Religious followers can only comprehend the god force from the spiritual experiences of others and/or books and teachers. Religion teaches limitation, awareness through others, things are done through the spirit of the prophet/savior, or holy man, which makes sense when you are operating out of the limitations of mind and body/indoctrination. The god force is spirit, freeing the soul is the awakening/actualization of the creative experience. Still encapsulated in the flesh but in the spiritual world, where all is one. Access to all is therefore at your disposal where the unseen is felt before it is seen. You acquire from the unseen which in turn manifest into physical reality when you can feel it. How can anyone teach you what is unseen? How can you be told what to see when it is made real by what you feel? Demanding/requesting in the visual/physical world is a blood sport (lust), a fulfillment of the senses, body and mind. Be very careful, the senses deceive from time to time. Stay conscious, honor the senses through a true sense of self. I can and will attract love through my imagination (spiritual mind) that strengthens and guides me, by saying no to everything negative, creating some beauty every day, and counting all costs. I AM forever grateful. I can and will attract all things through my imagination (spiritual mind) that strengthens and guides me, by saying "YES" to life, living my intention, planting some beauty every day, and counting all costs. I AM, one creator (the individual authority over my life and decisions), one Soul (the individualized consciousness of source energy), made from one blood, one flesh, one spirit. I AM at ONE I and my creator. (SOURCE) are one. All is one. the Way of Consciousness

(…)

Revolution is a forcible overthrow in favor of a new system. "The next revolution shall not be televised," -Gil Scott Heron. It is the inner revolution, awakening to my ideas. Inner Revolution is an invitation to remind us of our human right to achieve happiness for ourselves. It is a door to glimpse beyond that which we have been indoctrinated to believe, the freedom to pursue our own way. From the perspective of inner work, the honest thing to say would be something like "there are parts of my being that have nothing to do with you nor this created reality." Inner revolution is like a doctor assisting at the birth of a new life, an interaction within is bringing up parts of my untransformed self that will remove all impediments/blockages to my becoming. It is a labor that brings the hope of a better life into the indoctrinated/enslaved mind. A revolution is impossible without a revolutionary situation. I AM forever grateful. I can and will attract all things through my imagination (spiritual mind) that strengthens and guides me, by saying "YES" to life, living my intention, planting some beauty every day, and counting all costs. I AM, one creator (the individual authority over my life and decisions), one Soul (the individualized consciousness of source energy), made from one blood, one flesh, one spirit. I AM at ONE I and my creator. (SOURCE) are one. All is one. the Way of Consciousness

(…)

Everything is created through altered states of consciousness. Everything that manifests itself in your life is there because it matches the vibration from your thoughts. The web of energy commonly referred to as the "life force" or "soul" connects a stream of consciousness between all atoms and particles in the universe. Because of this, all humans and objects have an energy field that has its own vibrational frequency. As you experience the reality of matter to be vibration, you also start experiencing the reality of the mind everything, consciousness, perception, sensation and reaction. Focus, not prayer directs the energy, it's your superpower. Consistent prayer directs the focus, don't worry about tithes, pay attention. I AM forever grateful. I can and will attract all things through my imagination (spiritual mind) that strengthens and guides me, by saying "YES" to life, living my intention, planting some beauty every day, and counting all costs. I AM, one creator (the individual authority over my life and decisions), one Soul (the individualized consciousness of source energy), made from one blood, one flesh, one spirit. I AM at ONE I and my creator. (SOURCE) are one. All is one.
the Way of Consciousness

(…)

Life will never be perfect. Life is a spiritual evolution. The ultimate goal is self-realization. Successfully raising our spiritual vibration can only happen if we are willing to clean up any emotional wreckage. Trauma involving a troubled past, a lost love affair, or a divorce can block spiritual growth. Pushing it aside or creating a world where it does not exist ceases the evolution. The emotions associated with these events/unhealthy relationships block spiritual development. True intimacy and healthy connections with other like-minded people teach us how to be spiritual beings. For my growth I had to look at the people in my life and determine whether these relationships were good for me. Begin to mend your spirit with active healing techniques, positive lifestyle changes, nutrition, and even herbal medicine. The challenges are the journey. I AM forever grateful. I can and will attract all things through my imagination (spiritual mind) that strengthens and guides me, by saying "YES" to life, living my intention, planting some beauty every day, and counting all costs. I AM, one creator (the individual authority over my life and decisions), one Soul (the individualized consciousness of source energy), made from one blood, one flesh, one spirit. I AM at ONE I and my creator. (SOURCE) are one. All is one.

the Way of Consciousness

(…)

There is no need pondering who you will spend your life with until you acknowledge what you are going to spend your life for. I would like to spend the rest of my life for however long writing and inspiring others. It requires many hours of reading, research, continuing education, relationship building, travel, thoughtfulness, mindfulness, awareness, patience, alone time, and unconditional love. I get my inspiration from nature. I love to feed the birds, squirrels and rabbits that inhabit my domicile. The magnetism of nature calms and directs me. Walking in nature creates in me a kinship with all of life. I know the direction I want to pursue, the challenges, the downs, and the fulfillment that comes with my chosen course. When you/I decide how to spend the rest our lives and our life's work, it will make all future decisions clear cut choices. How is what I am asked, solicited, being faced with, tempted by, going to support my need and desire to be the best I can be at inspiring others/my chosen path? Inspiring others is the focus that must be supported for me to go all out. Inspiring another brings me a sense of happiness every day, if only just for a fleeting moment. This is the path I have chosen because it is right for me. I AM forever grateful. I can and will attract all things through my imagination (spiritual mind) that strengthens and guides me, by saying "YES" to life, living my intention, planting some beauty every day, and counting all costs. I AM, one creator (the individual authority over my life and decisions), one Soul (the individualized consciousness of source energy), made from

one blood, one flesh, one spirit. I AM at ONE I and my creator. (SOURCE) are one. All is one.
the Way of Consciousness

(…)

We are body, mind, and soul/spirit. Your **Soul is** your Higher Self, and it **is** your ultimate source of truth, peace, love, and freedom. The soul is the eternal part of you, given a body for the earthy sojourn, which is about removing the obstacles from the flesh and reveal the light of our Higher Selves. The soul lives in heaven (god consciousness) and appears to the blind body/flesh when we descend into the core of our beings, removing inner blockages, and undertaking the courageous task of healing, forgiving, understanding, empowering, loving ourselves and others. By listening to and learning how to embody our **Souls,** we mature on a soulful level and "Thy kingdom come on earth as it is in heaven." A soul's purpose is simply the Self-Realization of being the individualized consciousness of god. All things are possible to you in god consciousness I AM forever grateful. I can and will attract all things through my imagination (spiritual mind) that strengthens and guides me, by saying "YES" to life, living my intention, planting some beauty every day, and counting all costs. I AM, one creator (the individual authority over my life and decisions), one Soul (the individualized consciousness of source energy), made from one blood, one flesh, one spirit. I AM at ONE I and my creator. (SOURCE) are one. All is one.
the Way of Consciousness

(…)

Think in terms of energy. Consciousness is immaterial and cannot be divided. This implies that the only way to see god/SOURCE/the Universal life force/energy is as one. It is the sum total of all there is. To see and live in separation is to live out of the flesh/carnal mind. It is all one energy made up of atoms and molecules. The story/allegory of Eve being formed out of ATOM's (Adam) rib signifies the division of atoms/energy of the one in a portion of the limitless. Creation

71

is the splitting of the one energy into many forms. Underneath the superficial difference that divide us is the one spiritual energy that unites us. The universe is made up of atoms, the same ones in all of us. We are all cut from the same cloth. Albert Einstein said, "The splitting of the atom has changed everything except how we think." I AM forever grateful. I can and will attract all things through my imagination (spiritual mind) that strengthens and guides me, by saying "YES" to life, living my intention, planting some beauty every day, and counting all costs. I AM, one creator (the individual authority over my life and decisions), one Soul (the individualized consciousness of source energy), made from one blood, one flesh, one spirit. I AM at ONE I and my creator. (SOURCE) are one. All is one. the Way of Consciousness

(…)

The bible uses stories/allegories to depict the journey of the soul like momma used stories to articulate where babies come from. The allegories of the old testament are the indoctrination period, to keep you safe from all hurt harm and danger. In the old testament the shepherd/preacher guides the sheep. The new testament is the revelation period, it allows you to lift your head, lift thine eyes to the heavens, from which cometh the help, to make thine own way. The old testament reads you are a chosen people to build your self-esteem by following rules. The new testament reads there is neither Jew nor Greek, male nor female, black or white, all are chosen, love is the only rule. How long will you give a baby to walk? Until it does. So buy a pew, a cross to wear around your neck, but god forbid you see all people as one. Revelation knowledge will evolve you to see that love is the only rule, if karma doesn't get you first. I AM forever grateful. I AM forever grateful. I can and will attract all things through my imagination (spiritual mind) that strengthens and guides me, by saying "YES" to life, living my intention, planting some beauty every day, and counting all costs. I AM, one creator (the individual authority over my life and decisions), one Soul (the individualized consciousness of

source energy), made from one blood, one flesh, one spirit. I AM at ONE I and my creator. (SOURCE) are one. All is one. the Way of Consciousness

(…)

John the Baptist must be beheaded. The BIBLE is a collection of religious texts or scriptures sacred to Christians, Jews, Samaritans, Rastafari, and others consisting of parables and allegories. It is an esoteric/spiritual book about the human journey. In this particular allegory/moral story, John the Baptist being beheaded is you in this part of your spiritual journey. John the Baptist, the intellectual man/woman beholds the evils of civilization, condemns them and advocates for the punishment of evil doers. The death of John the Baptist refers to the passing away of the enthusiasm of character at the early age of our adult experience. This state is not a permanent state of consciousness, the state of consciousness that cometh after is mightier and permanent. Your consciousness state of John the Baptist must fall because it lacks the universal brotherhood of man and must allow for the descent of the spirit which removes the narrow comprehension of reform. Don't strive with evil. I AM forever grateful. I can and will attract all things through my imagination (spiritual mind) that strengthens and guides me, by saying "YES" to life, living my intention, planting some beauty every day, and counting all costs. I AM, one creator (the individual authority over my life and decisions), one Soul (the individualized consciousness of source energy), made from one blood, one flesh, one spirit. I AM at ONE I and my creator. (SOURCE) are one. All is one. the Way of Consciousness

(…)

There is no visual description of Nat Turner, or Joan of Arc, both freedom fighters, so why does color matter? We are a visual species and we respond to one another based on the way we physically perceived within the context of culture. Judaism is not a color it is a religion. Ancient Israelites, defined as those that wrestle/challenge god were brown. The only time color doesn't matter or is a problem is when the world's savior is portrayed as black. Why is that? Why won't the "TRUTH'" seekers of Christianity, the lovers of truth and righteousness set the record straight about a supposedly human being whose claim to fame was that he walked the earth as spirit and FLESH? Technology has advanced to the levels where we can employ science to accurately depict what historical figures looked like as if they were alive today. British scientists using forensic anthropology, similar to how police solve crimes, have stitched together what is probably the most accurate image of Christ's real face, and he's not the light-skinned figure many of us are used to seeing. Images of White Jesus have obviously been used to promote the idea that white is the best look for the world's savior. Why doesn't truth matter in the Church? Because it's all metaphor, allegory, opinion, perception, and belief. Whoever has the biggest gun wins. God bless the 2nd amendment, in guns we trust. I AM forever grateful. I can and will attract all things through my imagination (spiritual mind) that strengthens and guides me, by saying "YES" to life, living my intention, planting some beauty every day, and counting all costs. I AM, one creator (the individual authority over my life and decisions), one Soul (the individualized consciousness of source energy), made from one blood, one flesh, one spirit. I AM at ONE I and my creator. (SOURCE) are one. All is one.

the Way of Consciousness

(…)

The prefix to establishing my creative power in god consciousness is to understand who I AM. It's about figuring out who I AM and where I want to go. You can't take me there! The ONE, god/energy/SOURCE takes on all forms as the immaterial totality of all consciousness/existence. Atoms and molecules shift to create the intended visible shape and configurations of matter. It is how consciousness expands. When energy/matter takes on the form of humankind, it is in the consciousness of I AM. I AM/soul/individualized consciousness of god directs from within the god conscious

74

mind to expand into whatever/whomever it desires with the magic wand of focus. It creates/molds reality. All is a manifestation of mind. Rich man, poor man, beggar man, thief, I AM that in which I accept/believe myself to be. The I AM consciousness manifest on your behalf with intentional focused effort. What/whomever you believe you are at this moment the universe honors, with the simple prefix" I AM." No pun intended but I serve the same god Moses (the spiritual mind) served, the god I AM, which creates on behalf of my thoughts. Behind all manifestation are the ideas of mind. I AM forever grateful. I can and will attract all things through my imagination (spiritual mind) that strengthens and guides me, by saying "YES" to life, living my intention, planting some beauty every day, and counting all costs. I AM, one creator (the individual authority over my life and decisions), one Soul (the individualized consciousness of source energy), made from one blood, one flesh, one spirit. I AM at ONE I and my creator. (SOURCE) are one. All is one.

the Way of Consciousness

(…)

There are always risk in investing, however there is no learning without an investment. There is no love without an investment. And there is no knowing Source/the infinite/god without an investment. An investment is an act of devoting time, effort, and/or energy to a particular undertaking with the expectation of a worthwhile result. You have to make an expenditure to invest, a venture of self. You may lose but without the investment you will never win. It requires being vulnerable, taking a risk, a gamble, but you have to try it on/out if you are ever going to know whether or not something fits. You have to wear it. What are you afraid of? So I lose! As Jay Z so eloquently put, "You may fail a hundred times but you only have to get it right once." But then again I never lose, either I win or I learn, I never lose. I AM forever grateful. I can and will attract all things through my imagination (spiritual mind) that strengthens and guides me, by saying "YES" to life, living my intention, planting some beauty every day, and counting all costs. I AM, one creator (the individual authority over my life and decisions), one Soul (the individualized consciousness of source energy), made from one blood, one flesh, one spirit. I AM at ONE I and my creator. (SOURCE) are one. All is one.

the Way of Consciousness

(…)

The invisible realm is where all good and perfect gifts come from. It is the place where the visible is manifested.

When you request, seek, or invite a desire from the invisible realm/Father/subconscious mind, the question becomes how do you prepare as the gift moves from the invisible, when you can't see how it is coming? Preparing to receive from the invisible requires your actions and preparation to be invisible. You must act out of your invisible nature using those traits that are within you which are also invisible. The invisible intangibles necessary to stay every ready for reception from the invisible are all within you, many of which were used on the yellow brick road for Dorothy in search of home. It takes courage, intuition, LOVE, mindfulness, and all invisible tools within you. They also include other essentials hidden to the naked eye which you must possess, a will, focus, and trust in the invisible. (naked eye) Focusing on the invisible will create the visible. Heaven is within you. I AM forever grateful. I can and will attract all things through my imagination (spiritual mind) that strengthens and guides me, by saying "YES" to life, living my intention, planting some beauty every day, and counting all costs. I AM, one creator (the individual authority over my life and decisions), one Soul (the individualized consciousness of source energy), made from one blood, one flesh, one spirit. I AM at ONE I and my creator. (SOURCE) are one. All is one.

the Way of Consciousness

(…)

Where have you committed to go? The only thing you have to be certain of to get where you want to go is your state of mind. Being committed is a feeling of dedication and loyalty to that

76

which you are conscious of. There is always a complex of emotional and intellectual attributes that come and will determine the actions and reactions to your commitment. The biggest commitment you must keep however is your commitment to yourself. What dream have you committed to? It's always too early to quit. Whatever you give yourself up to, gives itself up to you according to its nature. Wherever you commit to go you first have to leave where you are now. You can't be both places at the same time, where you are and where you are headlining. One foot in the boat and one foot on the shore, something has to give. You have to leave shore (that which is familiar) and get on the boat heading to the other side (your destiny). Great changes may not occur right away, however stay committed in your decisions but flexible in your approach. Make your own space for what is important and it will grow and flourish. Then like Christ you will come into "your own city." Your own city is a metaphor for the manifestation of that in which you desire, the place you have chosen to consciously be.

Commit to yourself and consciousness/your state of mind will get you to the other side. I gotta get committed! I AM forever grateful. I can and will attract all things through my imagination (spiritual mind) that strengthens and guides me, by saying "YES" to life, living my intention, planting some beauty every day, and counting all costs. I AM, one creator (the individual authority over my life and decisions), one Soul (the individualized consciousness of source energy), made from one blood, one flesh, one spirit. I AM at ONE I and my creator. (SOURCE) are one. All is one.

the Way of Consciousness

(…)

Learn to master your moods and feelings.
Feelings and mood create reality. The feeling within gets the blessing/manifestation, it gives you your desired reality. The subconscious mind operates on feeling (hate, love, happiness, anger). When an impression, good or bad reaches the subconscious mind/Father it reaches there as feeling. And

whatever feeling reaches the subconscious mind/Father it creates more of that reality to grant your feeling request. Everything brings a feeling. Rejection, going on vacation is a feeling, having lots of money is a feeling, love is a feeling, losing is a feeling. What feeling are you searching for? We are vibrational beings, the feeling of your desires are honored by the Father/subconscious mind within you.

The Father/subconscious mind is blind, with no graven images (not an old white bearded white man in the sky) and no respecter of person (no chosen people). It's in you. Get the feeling, get the blessing. Learn to master your feelings. Things do not happen to you, they happen for you. I AM forever grateful. I can and will attract all things through my imagination (spiritual mind) that strengthens and guides me, by saying "YES" to life, living my intention, planting some beauty every day, and counting all costs. I AM, one creator (the individual authority over my life and decisions), one Soul (the individualized consciousness of source energy), made from one blood, one flesh, one spirit. I AM at ONE I and my creator. (SOURCE) are one. All is one.

the Way of Consciousness

(…)

The Christ/god part of you is hidden beneath the flesh. Underneath all those undealt-with emotions/problems which go to the subconscious/father/heaven, and grow there until they manifest as obstacles, negative people and terrible events in our life. When you remove ill feelings/obstacles and are at one with yourself, you experience the Kingdom of Heaven. The orderly adjustment of the divine within you. It is not a spatial expanse like Asia, Europe or America. It is not a continent that we call the Kingdom of God. It is the being of God that you recognize within you. The allegory of Jesus definitely located the kingdom of God (heaven) when it is said, "The kingdom of God cometh not with observation: neither shall they say, Lo, here! or, there! for lo, the kingdom of God is within you" (Luke 17:20, 21). It is peace within, it is the being of God. All is mind. The body/indoctrination dies at Golgotha (the place of the

78

skull). I AM forever grateful. I can and will attract all things through my imagination (spiritual mind) that strengthens and guides me, by saying "YES" to life, living my intention, planting some beauty every day, and counting all costs. I AM, one creator (the individual authority over my life and decisions), one Soul (the individualized consciousness of source energy), made from one blood, one flesh, one spirit. I AM at ONE I and my creator. (SOURCE) are one. All is one. the Way of Consciousness

(...)

Karma/the Law of Cause and Effect is the force generated by a person's actions and its ethical consequences to determine the nature of the person's next experience. The term refers to the spiritual principle of cause and effect, wherein intent and actions of an individual (cause) influence the future of that individual (effect), good intent and good deeds contribute to good karma, while bad intent and bad deeds contribute to bad karma. Bad karma works in direct correlation with an eye for an eye and a tooth for a tooth. Good karma can be perpetuated with one stroke of the golden rule (be kind and act with compassion). The core of the golden rule is a moral obligation to treat others ethically for our sake, not theirs. It takes valor. Valor represents strength of mind or spirit that enables a person to encounter hurt, danger and/or pain with firmness, personal bravery and courage. Valor is stability of the soul. We respond this way, not because of who they are but because of who we are. You know how to take one for the team, learn to take em for yourself. I AM forever grateful. I can and will attract all things through my imagination (spiritual mind) that strengthens and guides me, by saying "YES" to life, living my intention, planting some beauty every day, and counting all costs. I AM, one creator (the individual authority over my life and decisions), one Soul (the individualized consciousness of source energy), made from one blood, one flesh, one spirit. I AM at ONE I and my creator. (SOURCE) are one. All is one. the Way of Consciousness

(...)

Consciousness. All that is physical is a reference to matter, space, and time. These are the identities that are referred to as natural phenomena. A physical being is dependent upon the physical world from infancy. A physical being needs a physical god, a graven image, physical concepts, something they consider tangible for guidance/direction. All that is spiritual, the true you, not physical, reveals itself when the appetite for matter/the physical diminishes. The spiritual side of life is referred to the supreme soul, soul, spirit, sensation, breath, heaven, higher world, and the spiritual world, while the physical side of life refers to the body, brain, and heart. It has its purpose. The difference lies in your nature, your allegiance. The world proceeds from the one spirit housed in the body of man/woman. I AM a spiritual being. As a spiritual being, spiritual intuition guides. The world around you will change and you will be one step closer to total peace and happiness. I AM forever grateful. I can and will attract all things through my imagination (spiritual mind) that strengthens and guides me, by saying "YES" to life, living my intention, planting some beauty every day, and counting all costs. I AM, one creator (the individual authority over my life and decisions), one Soul (the individualized consciousness of source energy), made from one blood, one flesh, one spirit. I AM at ONE I and my creator. (SOURCE) are one. All is one. the Way of Consciousness

(...)

I AM where I AM by my own state of consciousness. I stay excited about life. Everything and everyone is happening for my benefit. We as individuals with free will choose our interpretations of reality. We decide what happens, and what it means to us. We can view everything as happening for our benefit, or going against us. Imagine walking through life and genuinely seeing everything that happens as beneficial to your success. Can you feel that power/ self-assurance/ and excitement that can come from this perspective? The powerful approach is to be happy and excited NOW. Today marks the
80

start of a new day, count it all joy. What beauty will you see? What challenges will you overcome? What progress will you have in pursuit of your dreams? Be in agreement with who you are conscious of being. Be excited about today without anxious dependence on the future. I AM forever grateful. I can and will attract all things through my imagination (spiritual mind) that strengthens and guides me, by saying "YES" to life, living my intention, planting some beauty every day, and counting all costs. I AM, one creator (the individual authority over my life and decisions), one Soul (the individualized consciousness of source energy), made from one blood, one flesh, one spirit. I AM at ONE I and my creator. (SOURCE) are one. All is one. the Way of Consciousness

(…)

Don't keep falling in the same hole over and over and over again. Get over it! What happened that you can't get over? Something happened in childhood that you can't get over? Mother/the teacher had their favorites? What happened in that love relationship that you could not get over? Get over it. What happened, happened and if you don't get over it, it will continue to happen. Don't let it shape your tomorrow. Until you get over it, you will be in the same relationship over and over again with different people, same energy. And you fight fire with fire until you get over it, an eye for an eye, a tooth for a tooth. Get out of that cycle. It can only leave you blind and snaggle toothed. When someone hurts you, don't go into denial, cry yourself a river, build a bridge and get over it. Shape your own reality, what lies ahead will be greater than anything you thought possible just like the past it is a matter of perception. The past is done just beyond the next horizon. Life is a self-offering, no baggage allowed. I AM forever grateful. I can and will attract all things through my imagination (spiritual mind) that strengthens and guides me, by saying "YES" to life, living my intention, planting some beauty every day, and counting all costs. I AM, one creator (the individual authority over my life and decisions), one Soul (the individualized consciousness of

source energy), made from one blood, one flesh, one spirit. I AM at ONE I and my creator. (SOURCE) are one. All is one. the Way of Consciousness

(...)

Do you talk about problems or solutions? Problems will develop you depending on how or if you go about solving them. Without problems we wouldn't grow, they make us strong. Whenever a problem you solve leads to another problem, it's probably not a problem to be solved but a truth to be accepted. A problem is a situation, question, or thing that causes difficulty, stress, or doubt. A problem is also a question raised to inspire thought. Use your imagination. Imagination brings forth possibilities/solutions/a means of solving a problem or dealing with it. If you focus on the problem the universe will bring you more problems, if you focus on a solution the universe will bring you more solutions. Address your problems head on. Sometimes the best way to solve a problem is to stop participating in the problem. Identify the problem but give your power and energy to a solution. Let thou be light! I AM forever grateful. I can and will attract all things through my imagination (spiritual mind) that strengthens and guides me, by saying "YES" to life, living my intention, planting some beauty every day, and counting all costs. I AM, one creator (the individual authority over my life and decisions), one Soul (the individualized consciousness of source energy), made from one blood, one flesh, one spirit. I AM at ONE I and my creator. (SOURCE) are one. All is one. the Way of Consciousness

(...)

Don't wait until you make the wrong decision, to figure out how truly important your decisions are. What is it that you truly want in life? Decide, deciding is the ultimate power. You will never leave where you are until you decide where it is you want to be. What you decide to do and to have is predicated on first deciding to do it, you have to wanna do it because a true decision is supported by action. Make your first decision today

82

to become a decisive person. Know exactly what you want and be willing to pay the price. Deciding is undergirded with discipline. Make decisions that prioritize your inner peace, know what you have to do, count the costs, and follow through. Your peace comes with knowing what is important to you, your realization. Decide what you believe and believe what you decide. Be not a product of circumstances but a product of your decisions, then all you have to decide is what to do next. I AM forever grateful. I can and will attract all things through my imagination (spiritual mind) that strengthens and guides me, by saying "YES" to life, living my intention, planting some beauty every day, and counting all costs. I AM, one creator (the individual authority over my life and decisions), one Soul (the individualized consciousness of source energy), made from one blood, one flesh, one spirit. I AM at ONE I and my creator. (SOURCE) are one. All is one.

the Way of Consciousness

(…)

I would like to introduce you to someone. Spirit is god, spirit creates everything. It allows you to walk and talk but you want a gold/wooden cross/calf/rosary beads that can't walk or talk, for what (foreplay)? Just till you figure out you house the god spirit. It is said, well-articulated, that god is spirit, the invisible defines the spirit, and we shall worship in spirit and in truth. There is only one spirit, so tell me who's spirit are you worshipping with when you worship in spirit and in truth? It is God's own spirit within you, there is none other. The spirit is able to be with every person in every place all at once on this earth. God is the indwelling spirit and only accessible from within. No name, no graven images, pure spirit. No one else can feel the spirit of god as you nor for you because it is only acknowledged through you. Go figure, the secret lies within the mind and creates for you with focus and consistency I AM forever grateful. I can and will attract all things through my imagination (spiritual mind) that strengthens and guides me, by saying "YES" to life, living my intention, planting some beauty every day, and counting all costs. I AM, one creator

(the individual authority over my life and decisions), one Soul (the individualized consciousness of source energy), made from one blood, one flesh, one spirit. I AM at ONE I and my creator. (SOURCE) are one. All is one.
the Way of Consciousness

(…)

Be clear on what is truly your concern. It doesn't matter what others think of you, it's what you think about yourself that the universe honors. Others can only judge from their own reality. Live in yours. The universe honors your thoughts. The Father /the subconscious mind is one with the infinite mind. Have a clear idea of how you should lead your own life as the infinite mind is about creating from the input of your desires. Know what makes you happy! Consistency and focus makes it happen. I AM about my Father's /the subconscious mind's business. If the conscious mind impregnates the subconscious mind with your desires from your thoughts, whose business are we really about when we are about the Father's /subconscious mind's business. Get a business to mind, then mind the Fathers/your business. Think it through to the end, live in the end. I AM forever grateful. I can and will attract all things through my imagination (spiritual mind) that strengthens and guides me, by saying "YES" to life, living my intention, planting some beauty every day, and counting all costs. I AM, one creator (the individual authority over my life and decisions), one Soul (the individualized consciousness of source energy), made from one blood, one flesh, one spirit. I AM at ONE I and my creator. (SOURCE) are one. All is one.
the Way of Consciousness

(…)

One blood, one flesh, one spirit. Flesh is the soft parts of the body and especially of a vertebrate. The parts composed chiefly of skeletal muscle as distinguished from internal organs, bone, and integument. It is the same flesh used for regular humans as for those considered gods. Blood is the red liquid that circulates in the arteries and veins of humans, carrying nutrients, oxygen
84

to and carbon dioxide from the tissues of the body. It is the same blood used for regular humans as for those considered gods. The spirit part is god, same spirit in everybody and everything. It's only one blood, one flesh, and one spirit. The only difference between those elevated to the highest levels in their spirit/god likeness and flesh followers is transcendence, led by focus, commitment and consistency. There is no separation in spirit/god. The part you feed the most wins. It ain't complicated, "The things which **I do you shall do** also; and **greater things** than these **you shall do" (John 14:12).** I AM forever grateful. I can and will attract all things through my imagination (spiritual mind) that strengthens and guides me, by saying "YES" to life, living my intention, planting some beauty every day, and counting all costs. I AM, one creator (the individual authority over my life and decisions), one Soul (the individualized consciousness of source energy), made from one blood, one flesh, one spirit. I AM at ONE I and my creator. (SOURCE) are one. All is one. the Way of Consciousness

(…)

Being made in the image of god, we are the crown of creation. Designed for success. All of us are made in the image of god/spirit. Return the favor. It is the indwelling spirit of god within each of us, that sustains us. I wish someone had told me the truth right up front. Fool me once shame on you, fool me twice shame on me. Today, I consider myself an unindoctrinated spiritual being housed in an earthly body suit. This suit is for the earthly sojourn designed by environmental factors prior to being indoctrinated with a programmed mindset for a sheltered designated upbringing. I felt like busting lose. Now, I AM a global citizen. I have matured beyond the safety net of cultural and class separation. I have received my sight. Here's the deal, god/spirit is invisible, housed in all persons. Enough said. I AM forever grateful. I can and will attract all things through my imagination (spiritual mind) that strengthens and guides me, by saying "YES" to life, living my intention, planting some beauty every day, and counting all

costs. I AM, one creator (the individual authority over my life and decisions), one Soul (the individualized consciousness of source energy), made from one blood, one flesh, one spirit. I AM at ONE I and my creator. (SOURCE) are one. All is one. the Way of Consciousness

(…)

At our present level of consciousness, we don't know it all nor will be able to do it all. We are structured as a very minute part of the All in All. We cannot see around the corner. However, we can be all we can be. It's not about where we have to go or what we have to achieve. It's not about doing, it's about BEING. Come in out the rain, it's an inside job. Be who you are, where you are and make the most out of every day. God incarnate is who you are (spirit embodied in Flesh), appreciate where you are. You don't have to do or look for anything, the universe expands automatically, magically, and we expand with it, stay prepared for the next great encounter. Treasure each moment, each encounter, be grateful. Everything can bring a small PEACE in life, don't miss it. One day we'll look up and it's all a memory. Be aware of the fullness being present in this moment brings. Look forward to seeing you again on the trail. I AM forever grateful. I can and will attract all things through my imagination (spiritual mind) that strengthens and guides me, by saying "YES" to life, living my intention, planting some beauty every day, and counting all costs. I AM, one creator (the individual authority over my life and decisions), one Soul (the individualized consciousness of source energy), made from one blood, one flesh, one spirit. I AM at ONE I and my creator. (SOURCE) are one. All is one. the Way of Consciousness

(…)

Our father who art in heaven is your spiritual source. It is the highest creative principle. Everything, including you began on the spiritual level. Make a decision to be all that you desire, it will convict you. Everything is first seen with the mind's eye, to be decisive, to be committed, to be loyal, to be faithful, to be true, to be loving, to be successful, and to be seen as a light for others you must first see yourself as that, it's a personal choice. Many times, we behave in ways that perpetuate what we have experienced. Don't seek who you want to become because of someone or something outside of you. The healer sees the cripple man walking. The healer sees the blind man with sight. Parents see what they want for their children. Decide how you see yourself, then design a path/plan. I AM a righteous man/woman, I AM successful, I AM a bright light ever expanding brighter. And that thought became a thing. I AM forever grateful. I can and will attract all things through my imagination (spiritual mind) that strengthens and guides me, by saying "YES" to life, living my intention, planting some beauty every day, and counting all costs. I AM, one creator (the individual authority over my life and decisions), one Soul (the individualized consciousness of source energy), made from one blood, one flesh, one spirit. I AM at ONE I and my creator. (SOURCE) are one. All is one.

the Way of Consciousness

(…)

I AM motivated because I have everything I need within me to allow my passion to feed my purpose. It meant finding an activity that keeps me engaged and putting forth effort. This self-motivation is the force that keeps driving us to achieve, improve, and advancing towards our goals and desires. Motivation means finding drive and direction from within. People who are motivated desire to do things, they desire to make a difference. Self-motivation helps us succeed. It helps us to learn and grow regardless how difficult the situation is. Fulfilling purpose doesn't come to you, you go to it. The man/woman on the top of the mountain didn't fall there. Action is the fundamental key. Nothing will work unless you do, trust the process and you will value the growth. Don't stop until you are PROUD. I AM forever grateful. I can and will attract all things through my imagination (spiritual mind) that strengthens and guides me, by saying "YES" to life, living my intention, planting some beauty every day, and counting all

costs. I AM, one creator (the individual authority over my life and decisions), one Soul (the individualized consciousness of source energy), made from one blood, one flesh, one spirit. I AM at ONE I and my creator. (SOURCE) are one. All is one. the Way of Consciousness

(…)

I AM is formless consciousness which creates out of desire with feeling/cherished ideals. Enter into the state of consciousness where all things exist. Three thousand years ago the earth was barren, bleak and lifeless with little vegetation. When you look at reality today you see skyscrapers, trains, planes, and automobiles. Where did it all come from? The Law of Consciousness is the law of god. All things exist in its relative state of consciousness/the invisible realm. All things were invisible in its relative state of consciousness before it was given physical manifestation (formed). You tap into the relative state of the thing desired with imagination/conscious focus which in turn impregnates the subconscious mind/subjective consciousness which creates form/the thing desired. The subjective consciousness is automatic, self-regulating, and self-acting. It acts out of that which you are aware of being/having. The I AMness creates form. Be conscious of who you are and what you desire. You are the doorway of manifested reality. I AM forever grateful. I can and will attract all things through my imagination (spiritual mind) that strengthens and guides me, by saying "YES" to life, living my intention, planting some beauty every day, and counting all costs. I AM, one creator (the individual authority over my life and decisions), one Soul (the individualized consciousness of source energy), made from one blood, one flesh, one spirit. I AM at ONE I and my creator. (SOURCE) are one. All is one. the Way of Consciousness

(…)

Get in where you fit in. The bible characters represent different levels of consciousness/unconsciousness. Every round goes higher and higher. How can you be happy when
88

materialistically some have more while others have less than you? Because deep down inside you know that you are more than the material reality. To worship in spirit and truth, you must first acknowledge that you are spirit first and foremost. What are you when the material possessions are gone? Let me hear that testimony, scream it to the rooftops! Like the biblical allegory/metaphor of Job from the land of UZ (Oz), no matter which state of consciousness I embody, the spirit/god is there. Working my way back to total consciousness, it's how the game goes. I AM forever grateful. I can and will attract all things through my imagination (spiritual mind) that strengthens and guides me, by saying "YES" to life, living my intention, planting some beauty every day, and counting all costs. I AM, one creator (the individual authority over my life and decisions), one Soul (the individualized consciousness of source energy), made from one blood, one flesh, one spirit. I AM at ONE I and my creator. (SOURCE) are one. All is one. the Way of Consciousness

(…)

You were so restless, anxious, and often unhappy, walking by sight when all things manifest from the invisible realm/spirit. God is spirit/energy. By thinking in terms of energy and by that I mean walking in the Spirit, something incredible happens. What the Bible calls "fruits of the Spirit" begins to grow in your life, peace, joy, love, faithfulness, and goodness, among other things. You become stable and develop your imagination, the ability to create desires from within. You become happy and receiving becomes a natural part of your life. You are no longer envious of others. Love frees your thoughts from the endless demands of your ego so you instead think about others and what might be good for them. Faithfulness becomes a part of your personality. You become trustworthy in everything you say and do. You become a new person. It is no longer accurate to say, "We are only human." Something completely new is born into your life so that you love, live, and help live. I AM forever grateful. I can and will attract all things through my imagination (spiritual mind) that strengthens and guides me,

by saying "YES" to life, living my intention, planting some beauty every day, and counting all costs. I AM, one creator (the individual authority over my life and decisions), one Soul (the individualized consciousness of source energy), made from one blood, one flesh, one spirit. I AM at ONE I and my creator. (SOURCE) are one. All is one.
the Way of Consciousness

(...)

Happiness is a feeling of contentment, that life is just as it should be. Perfect happiness, enlightenment, comes when you have all of your needs satisfied. Feeling is what the universe responds to. The universe does not know, care or visualize what you want in life. Your desires do that, good, bad, or indifferent. The universe manifests the aspirations of your happiness whatever they may be. That's why it is so important to count the costs. Having a purpose in life, fuels accomplishment, making it one of the fundamental factors of happiness. A purposeful person is someone who experiences frequent positive emotions, such as **joy**, interest, pride, and infrequent negative emotions, such as sadness, anxiety, and anger. While the perfect happiness of enlightenment may be hard to achieve, and even harder to maintain, happiness is not an either /or case. Without it, you'll live your life less focused, less efficient and you'll often feel restless and stressed because you won't feel aligned with the things you do. It is the feeling of what you are going after/doing that resonates with the universe/god, not the thing itself. The universe responds to the feeling to attain. To get, you have to feel good about what you already got. I AM forever grateful. I can and will attract all things through my imagination (spiritual mind) that strengthens and guides me, by saying "YES" to life, living my intention, planting some beauty every day, and counting all costs. I AM, one creator (the individual authority over my life and decisions), one Soul (the individualized consciousness of source energy), made from one blood, one flesh, one spirit. I AM at ONE I and my creator. (SOURCE) are one. All is one.
the Way of Consciousness

I find for myself that my first thought is never my best thought. My first thought is always someone else's (indoctrination), it's always what I've already heard about the subject, always the traditional wisdom. Learn how to think, use your imagination, it is the only thing that can take you out of the circumstances of what is already known. We're all influenced by our past experiences and when we attach negative labels to them, we subconsciously bring them into our present reality. Powerful thinking promotes powerful action. So think like this: Issue, thought, idea, vision, action. Take your thoughts and form an idea, then act. Moving forward, use powerful words that set you up for success in your thinking. Merely "trying" to move in another direction isn't motivating. Think to Master your next move, it's more motivating/purposeful. Think effectively and powerfully. I never lose, I AM still in the game, losing only comes at the end, when the game is over. If you are still in the chase, you can't lose, either you win or you learn to reassess. I AM forever grateful. I can and will attract all things through my imagination (spiritual mind) that strengthens and guides me, by saying "YES" to life, living my intention, planting some beauty every day, and counting all costs. I AM, one creator (the individual authority over my life and decisions), one soul (the individualized consciousness of source energy), made from one blood, one flesh, one spirit. I AM at ONE I and my creator. (SOURCE) are one. All is one.
the Way of Consciousness

Adults, it's time to go to back to school. It's time to retrain your mind to think differently about the world. It's time to embrace the reality that there is an unseen realm interacting in real ways with the physical world, and many children can see it. "Truly I tell you, unless you change and become like little children, you will never enter the orderly adjustments of divine ideas in man's mind (the kingdom of heaven)." Children have a natural inclination to see the world as **purposeful creation.** Everything has a function, when psychologists ask children why mountains exist; most say they exist, so animals have a place to climb. Children's imaginations are not limited by logic. They don't care what's real, if it is in their mind, it's possible! Children understand resources come from believing. We adults, on the other hand, have to be able to think things through logically in order for them to make sense. Engage, understand you first have to imagine it before you see it, feel good about giving your dreams and aspirations to the universe and understand all things visible were first invisible. I AM forever grateful. I can and will attract all things through my imagination (spiritual mind) that strengthens and guides me, by saying "YES" to life, living my intention, planting some beauty every day, and counting all costs. I AM, one creator (the individual authority over my life and decisions), one Soul (the individualized consciousness of source energy), made from one blood, one flesh, one spirit. I AM at ONE I and my creator. (SOURCE) are one. All is one. the Way of Consciousness

(…)

Everybody has a story, hopes, dreams, wins, losses, and lessons learned. We write our stories a page at a time. Your life is your message, so to be leader of your life, you need to decide what message you want to send. Naturally for you, me, and everyone else it's easy to succumb to the warmth and seduction of mediocrity. What most of us fear is not failure but success, it brings "all eyes on me." Every day, "all eyes on me," is setting an example for those around you whether you realize it or not, positive or negative. It is the life of a leader, fighting average, fighting ordinariness and complacency. A leadership mindset is one of awareness, and of course action to wake up daily and be aware of what's going on in your life. Lead by example. Once you've set your goals, ask yourself daily what you're doing to reach higher, to turn vision into reality. I AM forever grateful. I can and will attract all things through my imagination (spiritual mind) that strengthens and guides me, by saying "YES" to life, living my intention, planting some beauty every day, and counting all costs. I AM, one creator (the

92

individual authority over my life and decisions), one Soul (the individualized consciousness of source energy), made from one blood, one flesh, one spirit. I AM at ONE I and my creator. (SOURCE) are one. All is one.
the Way of Consciousness

(…)

Hurt people, Hurt people. Justice will remain an ever-receding horizon without full accounting of, and divestment from the spoils of white supremacy and the trauma it has caused. Either god is everywhere or it is not. Everywhere includes Buddhism, Islam, Hinduism, and everywhere else that is a part of everywhere (duh!) The systems and structures of white supremacy have been intimately joined with Christian supremacy, such that undoing white supremacy will also require relinquishing the images, ideologies, of Christian supremacy. The inability to acknowledge this at this time is part of the complex way we deal with trauma. We don't want to upset the PERPETRAOR. The acceptance of the traumatic reality presents in our system a key element in removing the effects of trauma, since what is denied cannot be faced and what is accepted is not explored. If trauma is left unaddressed, the person may suffer even more. It's therefore necessary for anyone who has experienced trauma to not only address the traumatic experience, but also learn to move past it. If not, hurt people, hurt more people. The first step is to focus on what we have learned from the trauma, if not those unresolved emotions go with you, today, tomorrow, and generationally: lynching, castrations, slavery, family separation, Jim Crow, segregation, today's Jacque Crow, mass incarceration, housing and job discrimination, the shooting of unarmed black men/women… LESSON LEARNED. Brutality against African Americans is/always has been a part of the American way of life since its inception in 1776. It's not about me it's about a system of injustice. Experiencing this trauma can cause a person to react in any number of ways so don't tell yourself (or anyone else) what you should be thinking, feeling, or doing because people react in different ways. Knowing and learning from the past opens the door to the future. Practice: issue, thought, idea, vision, action. I AM forever grateful. I can and will attract all things through my imagination (spiritual mind) that strengthens and guides me, by saying "YES" to life, living my intention, planting some beauty every day, and counting all costs. I AM, one creator (the individual authority over my life and decisions), one Soul (the individualized consciousness of source energy), made from one blood, one flesh, one spirit. I AM at ONE I and my creator. (SOURCE) are one. All is one. the Way of Consciousness

(...)

It is said "THE PEOPLE PERISH WITOUT A VISION." It didn't say the people parish without a church. Only the religion pushers/pimps perish without a church. The only vision a religion pusher /pimp can see is a bigger church for them, not a bigger house for you. What's your vision? Jump in the wave of vibrational harmony. Counter to the world of duality, unless thine eye become single (peace within), that which provides ones' happiness, the external source of ones' joy, will also be the source of ones' pain, it becomes the main source of ones' suffering. The church belongs to the world of duality (external joy). In the world of duality, all is two extremes of the same. To avoid the pain, identify and follow your vision, be happy with whatever comes. Go with the flow. Living in the flow is setting your goals but also giving space for things to happen from the unseen. Force nothing, let it happen, trusting that whichever way it goes, it's for the best. It's not your world, yet you are a small part, learn to coexist in it. You are an eternal soul. Let the universe show you what to do next. I AM forever grateful. I can and will attract all things through my imagination (spiritual mind) that strengthens and guides me, by saying "YES" to life, living my intention, planting some beauty every day, and counting all costs. I AM, one creator (the individual authority over my life and decisions), one Soul (the individualized consciousness of source energy), made from one blood, one

flesh, one spirit. I AM at ONE I and my creator. (SOURCE) are one. All is one.

the Way of Consciousness

(…)

The source of creativity is time with self. Forced labor created the time for privileged Americans to spend with self, using their imagination (spiritual mind), to be creative and inventive. When you have 400 years of slaves and servants to attend to your needs and necessities you have of plenty time for self. And with free labor, unearned income, one doesn't have to pay for trial and error. Most inventors and engineers have one common trait, they lived in their own world. According to the author of *The Call of Solitude*, solitude is an important and normal-part of human existence. And it's also essential for our best creative work. The best creative minds are flexible, and spend quality time working alone, but they don't ignore the value of other ideas. One can be instructed in society; however, one is inspired in solitude. In solitude we find peace, in peace we find inspiration. Imagination (spiritual mind) is your savior! Solitude is required for the subconscious to process and unravel problems. Life's creative solutions require alone time. I'm going to make time for my imagination (spiritual mind) in solitude and allow you to work for you while I work for me. Play fair. I AM forever grateful. I can and will attract all things through my imagination (spiritual mind) that strengthens and guides me, by saying "YES" to life, living my intention, planting some beauty every day, and counting all costs. I AM, one creator (the individual authority over my life and decisions), one Soul (the individualized consciousness of source energy), made from one blood, one flesh, one spirit. I AM at ONE I and my creator. (SOURCE) are one. All is one.

the Way of Consciousness

(…)

Truth, what you focus on expands. When we allow our thoughts to journey down the path of hate, hopelessness, envy, strife, despair, or anger, we are contributing our attention, our energy,

95

towards that which we don't want. We reinforce struggles and the conflict with our focus. You don't have to imagine magical powers. Your magical/super power is your focus, whatever you focus on grows, expands, and attracts more of the same. Can you shift your attention away from all that's going "wrong," to all the things around you that feel right? Speak it, what you speak becomes your reality. Speak your thoughts to life. Your words are vibrations that multiply thought patterns. Think, know what you want, speak it, focus on how it brings you joy and you can't go wrong. Take heed, feel the experience of the joy before it happens it will bring and that is what makes it happen. Think happy feelings. It is done unto you as you believe. I AM forever grateful. I can and will attract all things through my imagination (spiritual mind) that strengthens and guides me, by saying "YES" to life, living my intention, planting some beauty every day, and counting all costs. I AM, one creator (the individual authority over my life and decisions), one Soul (the individualized consciousness of source energy), made from one blood, one flesh, one spirit. I AM at ONE I and my creator. (SOURCE) are one. All is one. the Way of Consciousness

(...)

The unconscious person does what he/she has been taught. A conscious person is an individual who has claimed the right to freedom of thought. The level of your consciousness depends on the calmness of your mind. Consciousness lives in the present moment and adheres to being **careful, and diligent/surviving at** all present times. THE PRESENT TIME IS ALL THAT EXIST, it's all there is and will ever be. The brain does not do consciousness, consciousness does the brain. Consciousness creates, it is the consciousness that reflects the I AM, it is not the consciousness that thinks, but responds to obligation of your beliefs, which in turn dispenses outcomes. You got what you got, because you did what you did. Consciousness means being aware of and responding to one's surroundings in a beneficial way. A conscious person will eventually come to understand that the entire universe is his/her

96

surroundings, and it dispenses love, justice, karma and everything else, creating balance within the context of the immediate environment. Being **brave** and **honest** are great qualities for a human being to either receive or retain consciousness. The most positive personality trait that moves one beyond unconsciousness, to consciousness is unconditional LOVE. I AM forever grateful. I can and will attract all things through my imagination (spiritual mind) that strengthens and guides me, by saying "YES" to life, living my intention, planting some beauty every day, and counting all costs. I AM, one creator (the individual authority over my life and decisions), one Soul (the individualized consciousness of source energy), made from one blood, one flesh, one spirit. I AM at ONE I and my creator. (SOURCE) are one. All is one. the Way of Consciousness

(...)

The struggle is not real. The universe was built for us. Unclean the negative programming. Things do not happen to us; things happen for us. There is a law of faith and belief which is just as definite as any other law in nature. The spirit/energy unfolds from the unseen and this law is the Creative Principle of Life. Everything was first invisible before it became visible. "It is done unto you as you believe." Think about its meaning and you will discover that life only responds to your belief, and it responds after the manner of your believing, "as you believe." It is like a mirror reflecting the image of your belief. Habits of attention and perception create the experience we have in the world. Forget the artificial theology and doctrines of religion and look at life a different way, not through the lens of a "creator," but rather, a "creative force." God is not a man that god should lie. "God does not shoot craps or play dice with the Universe, neither should you. God is a force that must be reckoned with. All things work from positivism, not mysticism. I AM forever grateful. I can and will attract all things through my imagination (spiritual mind) that strengthens and guides me, by saying "YES" to life, living my intention, planting some beauty every day, and counting all costs. I

97

AM, one creator (the individual authority over my life and decisions), one Soul (the individualized consciousness of source energy), made from one blood, one flesh, one spirit. I AM at ONE I and my creator. (SOURCE) are one. All is one. the Way of Consciousness

(…)

The Christian religion as most religions is an anthropomorphic account of the universe. Anthropomorphism is the attribution of human characteristics or behavior to a god/force. There are three primal reasons why we might anthropomorphize God: we feel like the god force should recognize our physical problems, we'd like to be friends with the god force, or we can't explain god's unpredictable behavior. God is not a person, god is a force. That force is actualized in all things. Attributing human intent to god/ spirit/energy real or imagined, is one way that people make sense of the behaviors and events that they encounter. The Egyptians personified the god force as Ra, the Greeks Zeus, India Krishna, and the West as Jehovah/ Jesus/**I AM**. Just like the personification of giving with Santa, and courage with the lion, it makes one feel good to feel all knowing. Human relations with the god force have turned personifications of the force into truth and fixed ideas. Western theology has forgotten that these truths are illusions and worn-out metaphors without power. Positivism is what lines up with the force/energy/spirit and the greatest positive attribute is LOVE. The whole idea of addressing environmental issues, war, hunger and hate with a big man in the sky, mind you not a woman in the sky, has created the world we live in. I AM forever grateful. I can and will attract all things through my imagination (spiritual mind) that strengthens and guides me, by saying "YES" to life, living my intention, planting some beauty every day, and counting all costs. I AM, one creator (the individual authority over my life and decisions), one Soul (the individualized consciousness of source energy), made from one blood, one flesh, one spirit. I AM at ONE I and my creator. (SOURCE) are one. All is one. the Way of Consciousness

All things were first invisible before they were visible. And it isn't by magic, it's by focus. A Creator is a person that brings something into existence and uses focus to bring imagination into reality. HE/SHE brings the invisible to the visible. That which was not, now is. "Speak those things that were not as if they were." What say you? When things float in your head, they are part of the invisible domain, start taking out your thoughts and put them on paper so you can see what you have, what you can make with it. Then focus, concentrate your interest, which by default ignores many other things. Focus means saying no to all of the hundreds of other ideas that are there, pick carefully. They say, "A picture is worth a thousand words" and really focused people always have some sort of plan/vision to follow. They have a clear picture of where they're going and a reasonable idea of how to get there. Set up a structured path/blueprint and stay on course. I AM forever grateful. I can and will attract all things through my imagination (spiritual mind) that strengthens and guides me, by saying "YES" to life, living my intention, planting some beauty every day, and counting all costs. I AM, one creator (the individual authority over my life and decisions), one Soul (the individualized consciousness of source energy), made from one blood, one flesh, one spirit. I AM at ONE I and my creator. (SOURCE) are one. All is one.

the Way of Consciousness

To be free is a balancing act. It requires self-discipline. Don't crash and burn. Know that freedom has a twin brother/sister that goes by the name of responsibility. So pretend, find some core beliefs, make a vow, pledge to a military code of bigoted ethics, enlist, follow any culturally defined commandments/rules and regulations, join a church, pledge allegiance to a Baptist doctrine, a catholic doctrine, a flag, a nation, a gang, NA, AA, because freedom without love requires an indoctrinated mind to find its way around. Indoctrinate yourself with the wine of any

set of beliefs that will protect/hide you from yourself for freedom will be your demise without love, no limits. True freedom requires the responsibility/commitment of love. Without which you'll need something to commit to, to guide one's actions. Find something outside yourself to restrict and/or dictate your movements, it will allow you to have a shallow life without perceiving oneself as to being a shallow person. It will at least allow you to think you are not conflicted. The only problem is, most organized values don't allow for every human being to be seen as one of us. Every organization is built on a bias. Don't get it twisted, either you are a spiritual being that walks in spirit and in truth or you are an organizational biased being. God is the frequency of unconditional love, when you get to that you will get to god! Are you there yet? I AM forever grateful. I can and will attract all things through my imagination (spiritual mind) that strengthens and guides me, by saying "YES" to life, living my intention, planting some beauty every day, and counting all costs. I AM, one creator (the individual authority over my life and decisions), one Soul (the individualized consciousness of source energy), made from one blood, one flesh, one spirit. I AM at ONE I and my creator. (SOURCE) are one. All is one.
the Way of Consciousness

(…)

Joy and happiness consist in part with the anticipation of coming attractions. It's Friday afternoon, minutes away from quitting time, and the expectation of Virginia Beach has created an anticipation of fun, frolic in the sun, a weekend of pure pleasure. You see yourself hitting the waves and a feeling of joy abounds. "Be anxious for nothing." Anticipate and prepare. Anticipation is a feeling of excitement about something that is going to happen in the near future. When we anticipate, our brain enables us to make sound decisions that enhance our being in the world and keep us from acting in compulsive and destructive ways. When you anticipate something you want, even if you don't know what the outcome will be, you activate your brain's reward center, your brain releases feel-good
100

hormones. This helps to reinforce behaviors that are beneficial. Anticipation alerts all of the pleasure centers in the body and says wake up, which can create happy feelings. As you wait for approval when you know you nailed it, patiently waiting to see if they will like what you have created, you activate the reward system in your brain. Anticipation is the ultimate power, losers react, winners anticipate. Live your life in anticipation that something great is about to happen and it will. I AM forever grateful. I can and will attract all things through my imagination (spiritual mind) that strengthens and guides me, by saying "YES" to life, living my intention, planting some beauty every day, and counting all costs. I AM, one creator (the individual authority over my life and decisions), one Soul (the individualized consciousness of source energy), made from one blood, one flesh, one spirit. I AM at ONE I and my creator. (SOURCE) are one. All is one.

the Way of Consciousness

(...)

How can anyone tell you how to get where they have never been? Believe me, you will find something greater in the woods than in books. The door to the forest (destiny) is covered by trees but there is a way in and you have to wanna find it. To reach the heights beyond what is known by those that went before you, there is no blueprint/book, it's only a path. And the only way to the other side is through this vast wooded area (obstacles). It's not where you come from, it's about taking on new challenges, to get where you're going. Each day for me brings new expectation, a strong feeling that something will happen for my benefit leading to an unimaginable future. You can only imagine what you have been exposed to, that's why access and exposure denied is detrimental to the expansion of humanity. The gift of each new day brings forth new joys to unfold. Each sunrise gets me excited about discovering opportunities to expand upon the I AM, that I AM always growing in consciousness. I AM forever grateful. I can and will attract all things through my imagination (spiritual mind) that strengthens and guides me, by saying "YES" to life, living my

intention, planting some beauty every day, and counting all costs. I AM, one creator (the individual authority over my life and decisions), one Soul (the individualized consciousness of source energy), made from one blood, one flesh, one spirit. I AM at ONE I and my creator. (SOURCE) are one. All is one.
the Way of Consciousness

(...)

You are limitless without FEAR. Once you become fearless, you become limitless. Scientifically proven, we live in a limitless universe! Why are we limiting ourselves then? It's probably because it's the way the 1% indoctrinates the culture so they alone remain the 1%, the royal family. The god force is limitless and boundless, in everything and everyone simultaneously. It is the creative force of the universe and all the galaxies on the order of 100,000 in our local super cluster and an estimated 100 billion in all of the observable universe. There is so much unknown yet to be experienced. How is new music formed, what happened to inspire Duke Ellington and the Big Band Era, Motown, the Funk, New Jack Swing? By going beyond the limits of what was known at that time. All discoveries are stumbled upon on the way somewhere beyond what we now know, innovation is not already known. It is an adventure, if you knew where you were going it wouldn't be a discovery. Are you satisfied to follow what you know, study what you don't know, or are you on a path to expose yourself to what you don't know that you don't know? Take off the cloak of dogma and indoctrination, go outside the circumference of your current reality, live a life of no limits. I AM forever grateful. I can and will attract all things through my imagination (spiritual mind) that strengthens and guides me, by saying "YES" to life, living my intention, planting some beauty every day, and counting all costs. I AM, one creator (the individual authority over my life and decisions), one Soul (the individualized consciousness of source energy), made from one blood, one flesh, one spirit. I AM at ONE I and my creator. (SOURCE) are one. All is one.
the Way of Consciousness

Begin to believe in the power of your own thoughts. A thought is an idea or opinion produced by thinking, a function of the mind. But where do thoughts come from? It would be good to know because every thought has the potential to lead to an action, which is why it's important to interrogate our ideas. Physical reality will mirror back at you your thoughts in what you perceive, feel, and experience and not only influence your own life but the lives of those in your energy sphere (aura). The culture, the environment, the family, physical reality exposes you to your particular set of thoughts and beliefs. Beliefs make thoughts, thoughts create words, words create actions, actions become habits, habits create values, and values create destiny. Realize how powerful your thoughts are. A negative mind will never give you a positive life. Allow beautiful thoughts to build you a beautiful life. Write your own script and remember your lines. Speak those thoughts that were not as if they were. I AM forever grateful. I can and will attract all things through my imagination (spiritual mind) that strengthens and guides me, by saying "YES" to life, living my intention, planting some beauty every day, and counting all costs. I AM, one creator (the individual authority over my life and decisions), one Soul (the individualized consciousness of source energy), made from one blood, one flesh, one spirit. I AM at ONE I and my creator. (SOURCE) are one. All is one. the Way of Consciousness

(…)

Don't allow new or old desires to short circuit the dreams that have not yet been achieved. Why can't you hold your focus? Pay attention! "You are limited because of a shallow attention span and a lack of imagination." When you cannot hold your focus, you miss the shot, drop the ball, and send the wrong message. My mama used to say, "Don't let your eyes be bigger than your stomach." We all know, there is more where that came from, but what's the price? The universe is limitless, and the god force works through you on its own behalf. Just like you, it loves to expand itself. You paint a picture of what you have seen, then you want it. To do so, leave the past behind and grab hold of the wind. Where you end up will be beyond what you could ever have imagined. The desires/experiences you want to have, are envisioned by the imagination and the subconscious mind/holy spirit /god force, brings forth the reality you live, creates it. The god force brings everything into existence, stop trying to name it and get with it. Your job is to get with the beneficial thing needed for this moment for the next moment to benefit you. I AM forever grateful. I can and will attract all things through my imagination (spiritual mind) that strengthens and guides me, by saying "YES" to life, living my intention, planting some beauty every day, and counting all costs. I AM, one creator (the individual authority over my life and decisions), one Soul (the individualized consciousness of source energy), made from one blood, one flesh, one spirit. I AM at ONE I and my creator. (SOURCE) are one. All is one. the Way of Consciousness

(…)

Be above reproach, or you will pay a tax. There are many things in this realm of the reality that may and can excite you. But what is it that no matter where you go on this physical plane will be there to comfort you, that brings you joy, and makes life worth getting up in the morning? Focus on that! And it had better be held in a secret place where only you can unlock the box, for whoever gets the key becomes your master. Physical reality can be manipulated by natural disaster, excitement, envy, jealousy, or just plain old nastiness, and hatred. It can build up, let down, define, defame, make to cease and desist, put out, put you in a hole, or break you. However, I AM (being) is my connection to eternal bliss. I AM not made Ford tough, made by Mattel, Polo, Twitter, Union, VCU, VUU, connections, dead presidents nor you. I AM not built from sight/nothing outside of me, myself, and I, its vibrational. I can take on any weight, a pound at a time, weight builds muscle. I can't be disrupted, my smiley face comes from the inside out. I enjoy your company, but don't get it twisted, I AM at my happiest when you ain't here physically,
104

allowing my love/god force connection to be at its highest resonance, no interference. Stay above reproach, serve your ambition, vibrations are always welcome, distractors will have to climb. I AM forever grateful. I can and will attract all things through my imagination (spiritual mind) that strengthens and guides me, by saying "YES" to life, living my intention, planting some beauty every day, and counting all costs. I AM, one creator (the individual authority over my life and decisions), one Soul (the individualized consciousness of source energy), made from one blood, one flesh, one spirit. I AM at ONE I and my creator. (SOURCE) are one. All is one. the Way of Consciousness

(…)

If you really want to walk out of your aspirations and desires, make a conscious effort to do so each and every day. Prioritize your life, if you don't someone else will. Be concerned about what you are becoming, not what you are getting. Your walk is the most significant aspect of your life because you will attract what you are no matter what you have. If you ignore your walk or place other issues before it, you are likely to lose your footing. Old fashion rules and old fashion ideas can only confine, profound commitment to a dream does not constrain, it liberates. Attitude matters not beliefs. It's all about energy, positivism. Motivation and enthusiasm keep us positive about our goals and our lives. The sooner you realize where you are going, and who you are becoming, the sooner you realize where everything else belongs. In order to say yes to your priorities, you have to be willing to say no to something else. I AM forever grateful. I can and will attract all things through my imagination (spiritual mind) that strengthens and guides me, by saying "YES" to life, living my intention, planting some beauty every day, and counting all costs. I AM, one creator (the individual authority over my life and decisions), one Soul (the individualized consciousness of source energy), made from one blood, one flesh, one spirit. I AM at ONE I and my creator. (SOURCE) are one. All is one. the Way of Consciousness

(…)

You are more than what you believe at any given moment, a Christian, a catholic, a Jew, a Muslim, a Buddhist, a Hindi, etc. Your beliefs go far beyond what a particular religion has espoused, canonized or dogmatized. SOURCE is a neutral yet neutralizing force. It is the ultimate creative force whether you choose negative or positive, light or darkness. It will maintain balance (karma/Kinetic energy). As a human soul the highest level of individualized consciousness on this physical plane, you get to choose which works best for you based on your Kinetic energy level. In other words, what works best for you based on your current level of consciousness, to build up all of humanity or to tear down various aspects of humanity based on your ultimate beliefs? What do you believe about sex? What does your religion believe? What does it have to say about exercise? Guns? Marriage? Polygamy? Drugs? Human sacrifice? Hair styles? Swimming in bathing suits? Tattoos? Hip hop? Dancing? Being healed? Blood transfusions? All life being eternal? To be honest about it, now that I have a mind of my own, I'm just keeping the energy positive and doing the next right thing. I AM forever grateful. I can and will attract all things through my imagination (spiritual mind) that strengthens and guides me, by saying "YES" to life, living my intention, planting some beauty every day, and counting all costs. I AM, one creator (the individual authority over my life and decisions), one Soul (the individualized consciousness of source energy), made from one blood, one flesh, one spirit. I AM at ONE I and my creator. (SOURCE) are one. All is one. the Way of Consciousness

(…)

Wake up people. Thoughts create reality. Beliefs are not merely ideas that the mind possesses, belief possess the mind. Pay attention. It's not your beliefs that give you positive results, it's doing what's positive, the next right thing that is beneficial to all parties involved. Sometimes your beliefs will line up with what's positive, creating positive results and sometimes your
106

beliefs are negative and line up with negative results manifesting as suffering. KARMA does not care about your beliefs, it just balances the scales. KARMA is a universal law, the mechanism in which the universe balances itself based on the energy you put out. You had best critique your beliefs and not walk in blind faith. The allegory goes Joshua went into Jericho and killed a whole race of people without remorse so his people could eat. However, when Hitler did the same thing so his people could eat, it was a holocaust, go figure, you can't get by karma. I'm saying they were both violations of a people's sovereignty by definition regardless of your beliefs and whose side you're on. You inflict pain on a people because of your separatist views and its glory to god. When you suffer the consequence/KARMA of your beliefs, the same violence you inflicted it's a holocaust. Check your beliefs, just because you believe does not make it positive. Negative thoughts and action don't become positive based on who said it. Stay positive and your KARMA will be positive. I AM forever grateful. I can and will attract all things through my imagination (spiritual mind) that strengthens and guides me, by saying "YES" to life, living my intention, planting some beauty every day, and counting all costs. I AM, one creator (the individual authority over my life and decisions), one Soul (the individualized consciousness of source energy), made from one blood, one flesh, one spirit. I AM at ONE I and my creator. (SOURCE) are one. All is one.

the Way of Consciousness

(…)

Smoking is an example of an activity that once appeared positive for the smoker but has been found to have severe consequences. Cigarettes relax and produce weight loss. The nicotine in the tobacco suppresses the body's appetite and overall desire to eat for brief periods of time. One of the main reasons people take up or continue smoking cigarettes is because it relaxes them during stressful periods. However, people who smoke have 20-30 times the risk of death due to laryngeal cancer when compared to non-smokers. Like everything in the physical plane there are two extremes to everything except love. Count the cost, understand the consequences of your actions. What are the facts/consequences behind what you believe? Smoking relaxes, why? Because it requires deep breaths. So, it not the smoking that relaxes but the deep breaths. Swimming and yoga do the same thing because they require deep breaths without the side effects of cigarettes. Positivism or religion? Know the side effects. Positivism never killed anybody. I AM forever grateful. I can and will attract all things through my imagination (spiritual mind) that strengthens and guides me, by saying "YES" to life, living my intention, planting some beauty every day, and counting all costs. I AM, one creator (the individual authority over my life and decisions), one Soul (the individualized consciousness of source energy), made from one blood, one flesh, one spirit. I AM at ONE I and my creator. (SOURCE) are one. All is one. the Way of Consciousness

(…)

Become all that you can imagine. Work on your goals, read positive affirmations daily, or listen to your favorite music. Start to think more positively, and feed your mind and soul with positive words, positive people and positive things. Do something every day to get your brain into a good, happy, positive mind set. Unlike religion. Positivism is not a dogma, doctrine, or philosophy but a way to live, an attitude, and you still get into heaven (a state of consciousness where the soul and body are in harmony). And the only side effect is more positivism. Become what you are conscious of being, affirm it. Someone has already done what you are aspiring to do, to be and to have, be grateful for opportunities. In the college community what you are conscious of being is practiced through internships and residencies, create your own practice. It allows you to walk out that which you desire to be by being it. You are actually speaking /living those things that were not as if they were, with commitment, under guided instruction. Concentrate your mind to think positive thoughts. Pay attention to your life and your situation. Count it all joy. Remember that

108

even an unpleasant event when flipped can lead to a great lesson learned, which in turn, turns that negative into a POSITIVE! I AM forever grateful. I can and will attract all things through my imagination (spiritual mind) that strengthens and guides me, by saying "YES" to life, living my intention, planting some beauty every day, and counting all costs. I AM, one creator (the individual authority over my life and decisions), one Soul (the individualized consciousness of source energy), made from one blood, one flesh, one spirit. I AM at ONE I and my creator. (SOURCE) are one. All is one.
the Way of Consciousness

(…)

It has been said that god is everywhere. Can you really acknowledge god's presence everywhere? And god said, "Where shall I hide the divinity of man/woman?" Have you ever been to the god presence within yourself? I guess you love to travel. However, you cannot physically leave God from one place and go to another place where God does not exist because there is no place where God does not exist. God is omnipresent. God even exists in Hell, or in states of mind that are hellish. All is mind. When you leave this life, when your body passes away, it is not like you disappear and go somewhere else. You just awaken to what has always been there. But you don't have to die to awaken to this truth. The harmony of body and soul (heaven) is within you. The Presence is with you at this moment. Man/woman is god asleep. God is man/woman awoke. The Presence is so overwhelming it can create fear and anxiety. Accept the risk that must be taken to bring this awareness to you. Wake up! I AM forever grateful. I can and will attract all things through my imagination (spiritual mind) that strengthens and guides me, by saying "YES" to life, living my intention, planting some beauty every day, and counting all costs. I AM, one creator (the individual authority over my life and decisions), one Soul (the individualized consciousness of source energy), made from one blood, one flesh, one spirit. I AM at ONE I and my creator. (SOURCE) are one. All is one.
the Way of Consciousness

I would like to preface this writing by saying every path leads to god just as every path leads to your destiny, and the joint destiny of the planet. The current Western theory/theology of the god force comes out of the DARK AGES. The god force is everywhere, the ALL in ALL. The only question that prevails is what is your path, which path creates for you and yours the expansion of consciousness? The god force has two distinct sides that exist on the earth plane, consisting of both negative and positive energy. You have free-will to decide which path you will follow. The theory about a savior preconcludes that the god force is divine and I am not, therefore I need a barrier/savior between me and the god force. But the god force is me, it recharges itself through the night, keeps my heart beating, and lungs pumping. The soul (the individualized consciousness of the god force) is clothed in human flesh as man and woman, me! I AM DIVINE. The divine energy/spiritual world is all about affirmative expansion, what you call the negative only comes to create balance. It rights the ship to get it back on an affirmative course. POSITIVISM is your ticket to the light whether you choose to accept it. It requires giving up a whole lot of the family indoctrination (in-dark-nation), reluctantly of freely. NAMASTE, in the Hindi tradition means the god in me acknowledges the god in you I AM forever grateful. I can and will attract all things through my imagination (spiritual mind) that strengthens and guides me, by saying "YES" to life, living my intention, planting some beauty every day, and counting all costs. I AM, one creator (the individual authority over my life and decisions), one Soul (the individualized consciousness of source energy), made from one blood, one flesh, one spirit. I AM at ONE I and my creator. (SOURCE) are one. All is one.

the Way of Consciousness

(...)

You are the main character. You are the ONE in your storied life. You are the source of your reality. Being the one requires

110

making the choices to suit where you are going, and it is the most important aspect of your earthly sojourn. No god in the sky is going to tell you what kind of car to drive. What to wear today. Your mental functioning at any given moment occurs under the constraints of the processing potential available at any given age. The self-awareness and self-regulation develops systematically, making more intelligent choices and decisions with maturity. In the classic, *The Wizard of Oz,* at every fork in the yellow brick road, Dorothy made a choice in direction, call it intuition, it's another of our superpowers. In the *Matrix*, Neo (the ONE) is faced with the choice of saving Trinity or saving humanity, life choices require mental focus. Be brave and bold with the choices you make. Make positive choices on a daily basis so that you may live an authentic life that is true to who you want to be. Choices are the hinges of destiny. Focus on the information needed for where you want to go, while filtering out irrelevant information. It is through our decisions not our conditions that we accomplish our aspirations. Relax, put your dream on Google Maps, then cruise control. I AM forever grateful. I can and will attract all things through my imagination (spiritual mind) that strengthens and guides me, by saying "YES" to life, living my intention, planting some beauty every day, and counting all costs. I AM, one creator (the individual authority over my life and decisions), one Soul (the individualized consciousness of source energy), made from one blood, one flesh, one spirit. I AM at ONE I and my creator. (SOURCE) are one. All is one.

the Way of Consciousness

(…)

Believe you deserve it, and the universe will serve it. Learn how to use your mind in which exist the stage of your imagination. Perceive with the mind's eye and discern mentally. See your desires. Everything in the visible realm was first a pictured thought in the invisible realm. The fruits of your life will manifest from the tree of your mind. You have to see it and believe it before you receive it. What you see is what you get. Health, wealth, and a fulfilled life will appear as you see it to be. Make a clear decision. Decision is the starting point of getting what you want. Decide!!! Decide where you want to go, find someone who has already done it, been there, and then hit Google Maps, stay the course and anticipate the manifestation. Wear the feeling of receiving just as you did on Christmas Eve as a child. The capacity to mentally experience the state you desire creates the reality. The feeling of you receiving that which you desire invokes the manifestation of the desire. I AM forever grateful. I can and will attract all things through my imagination (spiritual mind) that strengthens and guides me, by saying "YES" to life, living my intention, planting some beauty every day, and counting all costs. I AM, one creator (the individual authority over my life and decisions), one Soul (the individualized consciousness of source energy), made from one blood, one flesh, one spirit. I AM at ONE I and my creator. (SOURCE) are one. All is one.

the Way of Consciousness

(…)

The destiny and purpose of it all is to evolve from the unseen side of life. Evolving can be defined as the continuous growth of consciousness. Evolving is a continuous upward spiraling of consciousness that pulls humanity, nature, planets, suns, solar systems, galaxies and the Universes back into the divine blueprint. The blueprint is answering the call to creativity. Creativity requires a constant flow of energy that responds to source energy, through the invisible realm by physical manifestations. Everything comes and goes and is made to flow. Hurt/hate/harm stifles/disrupts the steady and continuous current of creativity. They have no place in the tree of life. Hurt is to feel or cause pain. Hate is intense or passionate dislike. It not only consumes a person, it affects their health, their sleep, their relationships, and hurts the person. It does nothing to the one that is being hated. Harm is physical or mental injury, especially that which is deliberately inflicted. The scars of hurt/hate and harm tells the story of where you have been, don't let it write the story of where you are going. Let it go, it's the only way to win the fight. I AM forever grateful. I can and will

112

attract all things through my imagination (spiritual mind) that strengthens and guides me, by saying "YES" to life, living my intention, planting some beauty every day, and counting all costs. I AM, one creator (the individual authority over my life and decisions), one Soul (the individualized consciousness of source energy), made from one blood, one flesh, one spirit. I AM at ONE I and my creator. (SOURCE) are one. All is one.
the Way of Consciousness

(…)

Use all the details and all of your life experiences to define and create yourself, it's all connected. Live your life through your god given abilities. There will be mistakes, mishaps, and downfalls but you only have to be right once. Invest in you. Believe in what you are doing. Every day you go to work and pick the cotton while those utilizing their imagination make the cotton into T-shirts (metaphor). Step out and focus on one thing. You can't explain how it is gonna work out, because the universe brings your dreams (unseen reality) to you through your imagination (unseen realty). You don't have to explain your life, you have to live your life. Destiny may be a mile but you will receive one city block at a time, make sure you pay attention to the details, while maintaining your sense of self. Too much too fast will take you out. What you give to yourself each day is valued in your own sense of worth, based on your own sense of self. Your mind is the promised land, and the chosen people is a metaphor for your chosen thoughts. I AM forever grateful. I can and will attract all things through my imagination (spiritual mind) that strengthens and guides me, by saying "YES" to life, living my intention, planting some beauty every day, and counting all costs. I AM, one creator (the individual authority over my life and decisions), one Soul (the individualized consciousness of source energy), made from one blood, one flesh, one spirit. I AM at ONE I and my creator. (SOURCE) are one. All is one.
the Way of Consciousness

(…)

What shall I do today? Do something today that your future self will thank you for. Source/god gives me this day, not a named day of the week. What I do with my day is my free will choice. Man labels the days in a sequential order for his/her purposes, not necessarily the purposes of SOURCE/god or me. Following a regimented order of purposed chores is contrary to the ever evolving /expanding/unfolding way of nature/consciousness. Be anxious for nothing. Each day has its own reward. I was indoctrinated away from this but soon I will fly free. SOURCE gives us this day to discover new realities. Each day unfolds according to the divine blueprint, they were not named. Don't allow the name to dictate your day. Make today, this day worth remembering beyond its name. Every day is a new beginning, and with that freedom comes a responsibility to SOURCE and self. Plant. If you stumble, make it part of the dance. All the flowers of all the tomorrows are in the seeds of today. Enjoy today, it will never come again. I AM forever grateful. I can and will attract all things through my imagination (spiritual mind) that strengthens and guides me, by saying "YES" to life, living my intention, planting some beauty every day, and counting all costs. I AM, one creator (the individual authority over my life and decisions), one Soul (the individualized consciousness of source energy), made from one blood, one flesh, one spirit. I AM at ONE I and my creator. (SOURCE) are one. All is one.

the Way of Consciousness

(…)

SOURCE re-enforces focus, and now I want SOURCE every day. I think higher, I think better. It changed my life, I feel so free, I feel so happy. The child/carnal mind believes what you can see is more important than what you can imagine. "A bird in hand is worth 2 in the bush." However, once you receive what you wished upon a star, and a profound truth has been seen, it cannot be "unseen". There's no going back to the person you were. I'm going with unseen reality. I believe in unseen realty. What I see will be part of the planets coming attractions. I will bring my thoughts to life with FAITH. Faith is believing in me,

114

it's turning dreams into deeds, its betting on myself. Belief is following something or someone else. Faith is being loyal to myself! Close your eyes when you dream. Then weave unseen reality into form, it can't let you down, it is limitless. It consists of all of the options. I AM forever grateful. I can and will attract all things through my imagination (spiritual mind) that strengthens and guides me, by saying "YES" to life, living my intention, planting some beauty every day, and counting all costs. I AM, one creator (the individual authority over my life and decisions), one Soul (the individualized consciousness of source energy), made from one blood, one flesh, one spirit. I AM at ONE I and my creator. (SOURCE) are one. All is one. the Way of Consciousness

(…)

Life is a continuous exercise in creative problem solving. In times of difficulty, who do you call on? What better way to learn how to solve a problem than with a PROBLEM? What better way to gain strength than by lifting weights/exercise? You don't want to be my problem.

I'm learning to call on my IMAGINATION to deal with and overcome difficulty/complications. I AM the answer. When man had the issue of scorching heat burning his feet in the desert sand, he/ she found a way to protect their feet, shoes. When humankind wanted to solve the problem washing and bathing in the river with gators, bathtub. Life consist of solving problems, it's the way we expand or not. IMAGINATION is your savior; it will never leave you nor forsake you. It was given at birth to solve your problems, you have to turn away from it. Who told you that you were supposed to never stop calling on first your earthly support system? Those that never grew in stature to co-creators. If there is a problem, there is a solution, and if there is a solution therein lies progress. Use your spiritual support system to solve your problems. Pretend that life is one big math problem, and you have to find a solution. Identify problems but give your power and energy to the solutions. I AM forever grateful. I can and will attract all things through my imagination (spiritual mind) that strengthens and guides me,

by saying "YES" to life, living my intention, planting some beauty every day, and counting all costs. I AM, one creator (the individual authority over my life and decisions), one Soul (the individualized consciousness of source energy), made from one blood, one flesh, one spirit. I AM at ONE I and my creator. (SOURCE) are one. All is one.
the Way of Consciousness

(…)

We are the masters of our thoughts and oftentimes the slaves of our emotions. There are always emotions behind "I don't care," and pain behind "It's okay". One of the hardest things in life is to express our true feelings. Don't allow people and circumstances to shape your life by default. When you get to the end of your rope, what is your go to feeling? Is it working for you? Feelings are like visitors, they come and go. The difficulty lies not so much in developing happy feelings as in escaping from the old feelings. Tell your old feelings how to feel. Let the weak say I AM strong. Our feelings show the way to the most genuine path. Don't ever let feeling affect your reasoning. Change your frame of thought by building a different set of tracks laid down with new ways of facing challenges. I AM forever grateful. I can and will attract all things through my imagination (spiritual mind) that strengthens and guides me, by saying "YES" to life, living my intention, planting some beauty every day, and counting all costs. I AM, one creator (the individual authority over my life and decisions), one Soul (the individualized consciousness of source energy), made from one blood, one flesh, one spirit. I AM at ONE I and my creator. (SOURCE) are one. All is one.
the Way of Consciousness

(…)

Who is my neighbor? Your social-cultural system of designated behaviors and practices, morals, beliefs, worldviews, texts, and ethics will prescribe to your humanity how to act in any given situation within the brotherhood and sisterhood of humanity. And you and I, as our own moral authority, get to decide who

116

is worthy to be accepted unconditionally as neighbor. Moral behaviors are commonly mandated by the majority, the behaviors are but rehearsals of a culturally biased script. What you rehearse will be the outward expression of that which has been internalized/rehearsed. Unconditional love is not a performance, it is an expression of character. It's hard to act out of your heart/love when it isn't part of a daily rehearsed programming. Six days out of the week, we watch the chosen people, Rambo, Batman, and Superman destroy the unrighteous by the same means the unrighteous uses to destroy them and one day out of the seven forgiveness and turning the other cheek is practiced. You can't stop killing with killing, hate with hate. We constantly see and engage those without the one day a week script. We uphold punitive rather than restorative justice, we judge, and we condemn. Learn to uphold to the limits of unconditional LOVE every day. LOVE is not told what to do, it expresses itself. LOVE is the highest vibration, Rehearse love. I AM forever grateful. I can and will attract all things through my imagination (spiritual mind) that strengthens and guides me, by saying "YES" to life, living my intention, planting some beauty every day, and counting all costs. I AM, one creator (the individual authority over my life and decisions), one Soul (the individualized consciousness of source energy), made from one blood, one flesh, one spirit. I AM at ONE I and my creator. (SOURCE) are one. All is one. the Way of Consciousness

(…)

The Mind is the filter through which your total experience passes, and your emotions are the energy charge associated with materializing your experience as a result of passing through the mind. I AM/my mind is the door, the way in which all my experiences take place. It is a result of the first of the 7 Universal Laws, the Law of Mentalism, which declares that **All is Mind**. My physical reality, therefore, can only ever be a projection of Universal Consciousness, taking place in that portion of the universal Mind called I AM (me). I and my Father (SOURCE/GOD) are one. This principle embodies the truth

117

that "it is done unto me as I believe." It explains that THE ALL in ALL, the outward manifestations and appearances which are described as "The Material Universe", the Phenomena of Life," "Matter," or "Energy, comes from within the universal /individual mind. All is one. "ENERGY + VIBRATION (your state of consciousness/happy feeling) –MATTER (physical manifestation). THOUGHT + VOICE (gas) + FOCUS (liquid condensation)-Reality (solid). Hold that THOUGHT! Good or bad it has to manifest by Universal Law I AM forever grateful. I can and will attract all things through my imagination (spiritual mind) that strengthens and guides me, by saying "YES" to life, living my intention, planting some beauty every day, and counting all costs. I AM, one creator (the individual authority over my life and decisions), one Soul (the individualized consciousness of source energy), made from one blood, one flesh, one spirit. I AM at ONE I and my creator. (SOURCE) are one. All is one.

the Way of Consciousness

(…)

I AM forever grateful. The only way to change your thinking and emotions is to change your awareness. "Wives be subject to your husbands." This esoteric, an allegorical saying, parable. The wife represents the feminine subconscious mind that is impregnated by the husband/masculine conscious mind from exposure to the surrounding environment. Data is inputted on the keyboard from the Material Universe and the results are thrown up on the monitor screen of the subconscious mind. Whatever is focused on becomes a manifested desire. This is how the mind works, information is taken in via some outside stimulus from the environment and the results are thrown up instantaneously into the consciousness. Be choosy with the thoughts your subconscious mind processes and sustain a regular gratitude practice. You are the filter for those thoughts that enter the mind, and you have the power to influence them. Practice meditation, repeating positive affirmations of positive visualization to control your subconscious. This is how to subject the wife (subconscious mind) to the husband (conscious
118

mind) to create the reality you desire. I AM forever grateful. I can and will attract all things through my imagination (spiritual mind) that strengthens and guides me, by saying "YES" to life, living my intention, planting some beauty every day, and counting all costs. I AM, one creator (the individual authority over my life and decisions), one Soul (the individualized consciousness of source energy), made from one blood, one flesh, one spirit. I AM at ONE I and my creator. (SOURCE) are one. All is one.

the Way of Consciousness

(…)

The rays of the sun are not the sun but carry the energy of the sun that gives our life energy. So did the sun do it or the rays of the sun? Consciousness is not god however consciousness gives and sustains life from god the same as the sun's rays radiate from the sun. Consciousness is the form of god within us. We are all "made of **God**", or in other words, **Consciousness**. The infinite consciousness is the source of everything. Within our being is the essence of universal Intent. That Intent prompts us to create, to grow, to increase our knowledge and become ever more than before. This is the impulse of evolution in all living beings. So, did the Wright brothers invent the airplane or did they tap into the infinite mind of god/ the universal consciousness where all things exist and bring the plane into reality? How did they pull an airplane from the invisible realm? Consciousness is the awareness that lives within us all, that allows us to think, imagine, feel, analyze and interpret information. We have become so accustomed to these abilities that we no longer see the magic in them. Just like cable and the internet, the infinite mind is available to all. I AM forever grateful. I can and will attract all things through my imagination (spiritual mind) that strengthens and guides me, by saying "YES" to life, living my intention, planting some beauty every day, and counting all costs. I AM, one creator (the individual authority over my life and decisions), one Soul (the individualized consciousness of source energy), made from

one blood, one flesh, one spirit. I AM at ONE I and my creator.
(SOURCE) are one. All is one.
the Way of Consciousness

(…)

The war ends when one is all and all is one.

Instead of competing try planting.

Everything outside of nature comes out of the human imagination: your shoes, the socks the shirt you wear, the automobile, the airplane, everything in Lowes, Home Depot, Staples and Walmart came out of an individual's imagination. What gift to humanity/commodity is coming out of yours? PLANT!

Our challenges are the impetus for us to create, not fear. A man was walking barefoot on the desert, his feet were hot and burning. He could of, would of, should of, cursed the journey based on the challenge but he said ah ha! Sandals!

A woman was taking a bath in the river. An alligator was seen on the horizon, see was terrified!
She went days without a bath, and then she said ah ha! Bathtub!

Don't speak fear, anxiety, and/or frustration to problems. Speak ah ha! Speak solutions to problems.

The allegorical Abraham means FAITH. FAITH is belief in unseen realty. Unseen reality is imagination. Imagination is the gift that keeps on giving. Given at birth to all, and we didn't have to get baptized, circumcised or pay tithes get it. In times of indecision, Imagination is your knight in shining armor. Speak those these that were not as if they were (imagine). Visualize the results/outcome you desire. It is done unto you as you believe.

I AM forever grateful. I can and will attract all solutions to my challenges through my imagination (spiritual mind) that strengthens and guides me, by saying "YES" to life, living my intention, planting some beauty every day, and counting all costs. I AM, one creator (the individual authority over my life and decisions), one Soul (the individualized consciousness of source energy/god), made from one blood, one flesh, one spirit. I AM at ONE I and my creator. (SOURCE) are one. All is one. the Way of Consciousness

(...)

CONSCIOUSNESS IS MORE THAN ENOUGH

PAUSE

(…)

REFLECT

Nothing is impossible to a mind organized in positive beliefs

(…)

E=MC2

Think in terms of energy, frequency and vibration

POSITIVISM

www.agatheringof the ways.org